MAKING GOOD:
LAW AND MORAL REGULATION IN CANADA,
1867–1939

Young Canada was often portrayed as a virginal woman or as a healthy frontiersman, and the ideals of purity, industry, and self-discipline were celebrated as essential features of the Canadian identity. To ensure that Canadians lived up to this image, different levels of government passed a variety of laws and created an expanding range of institutions to enforce them. *Making Good* looks at the changing relationship between law and morality in Canada during a critical phase of nation-building, from Confederation to the onset of the Second World War. The authors argue that, though the law played a significant role in giving Canada a moral cast, its homogenizing tendencies did not always meet with anticipated success, as values deemed 'good' by the government were constantly repudiated by those on whom they were imposed.

Strange and Loo examine both the major institutions which patrolled morality – the Department of Indian Affairs, the Ministry of Justice, and the North-West Mounted Police – and the agencies that worked at local levels, such as police forces, schools, correctional facilities, juvenile and family courts, and morality squads. They also look at many fascinating acts of resistance to moral ordinances, showing that not all Canadians shared the same vision of goodness. Among the themes that run throughout the book are the concept of the internal threat to the foundations of national decency, the influence of the United States on Canada's moral order, and the regional discrepancies in the success of moral governance.

Through topics as diverse as gambling, marriage and divorce, and sexual deviance, *Making Good* shows that character-building was critical to the broader project of nation-building. The book will be a welcome addition to undergraduate courses in Canadian history, and will interest social historians; historians of Native peoples, the working class, and women; criminologists; and political scientists.

(Themes in Canadian Social History)

Carolyn Strange is an assistant professor at the Centre of Criminology, University of Toronto, and author of *Toronto's Girl Problem: The Perils and Pleasures of the City, 1880–1930*. **Tina Loo** is an associate professor of history at Simon Fraser University, and author of *Making Law, Order, and Authority in British Columbia, 1821–1871*.

THEMES IN CANADIAN SOCIAL HISTORY

Editors: Craig Heron and Franca Iacovetta

CAROLYN STRANGE and TINA LOO

Making Good: Law and Moral Regulation in Canada, 1867–1939

UNIVERSITY OF TORONTO PRESS
Toronto Buffalo London

© University of Toronto Press Incorporated 1997
Toronto Buffalo London

Printed in Canada

ISBN 0-8020-0884-4 (cloth)
ISBN 0-8020-7869-9 (paper)

Canadian Cataloguing in Publication Data

Strange, Carolyn, 1959–
   Making good : law and moral regulation in Canada,
   1867–1939

   (Themes in Canadian social history)
   Includes index.
   ISBN 0-8020-0884-4 (bound)   ISBN 0-8020-7869-9 (pbk.)

   1. Law and ethics.   2. Canada – Moral conditions – History.
   3. Law – Canada – History.   I. Loo, Tina Merrill, 1962– .
   II. Title.   III. Series.

   KE417.M67S87 1997   340'.112'0971   C97-930167-X
   KF345.S87 1997

University of Toronto Press acknowledges the financial
assistance to its publishing program of the Canada Council
and the Ontario Arts Council.

FOR MICKY

Contents

Acknowledgments

The names that accompany the title of this book refer to only two of the people who had a hand in *Making Good*. It is our pleasure to acknowledge the behind-the-scenes contributors to the book.

We are indebted to Craig Heron and Franca Iacovetta, who first approached us with the idea of writing something about law and moral regulation. As the front-line editor, Craig offered warm support that more than made up for his breathtaking ability to pare text. Through his criticism we learned a great deal, not the least of which was how to write a textbook.

With a stroke of foresight, we decided that it would be ideal to write in a bucolic setting. Gerry Hallowell, our senior editor, graciously allowed us to sojourn in the rustic surroundings of Blue Rocks, in Nova Scotia. He provided us with peace when we needed it, companionship when we sought it, and enough firewood to keep us from freezing.

Two researchers, Catherine Carstairs and Elsbeth Heaman, produced literature reviews on subjects as wide-ranging as temperance, child-labour law, and opium. In the process they provided us with more time to read and synthesize.

Another enormous debt is the one we owe to the historians whose work we have mined for this book. As footnotes were to be avoided in the books in this series, we have cited in the text those on whose work we relied the most. Historians whose writing informs our analysis are noted in the list of references. Two scholars, Tamara Myers and Margaret Little, were especially generous in sharing their unpublished work. We are also grateful for the anonymous reader whose comments saved us from several inexcusable infelicities.

Our final debt is one that no one other than ourselves will recognize. Writing is a pleasure when words come easily, but it is a delight when it is a truly collaborative project, shared with a colleague and friend.

MAKING GOOD:
LAW AND MORAL REGULATION IN CANADA,
1867–1939

Introduction

What's Law Got to Do with It?

Law's connection to morality is ancient. Originally expressed in religious codes, laws relating to morality were packaged with regulations governing a wide range of prohibited behaviour. According to the Ten Commandments, for instance, Hebrews were not to kill or steal, but also not to commit adultery or to worship idols. The current-day Canadian Criminal Code, a much more comprehensive statute, is similar to that ancient code of law in many respects: it defines penalties for a broad range of offences (among other things, crimes against the person, and property offences), and it pronounces certain breaches of morality illegal.

The most significant difference between legal forms of regulation, such as criminal codes, and religious edicts is that, in the former, the state, and not a divinity, is the prime authority. Furthermore, not even the most copious criminal statutes encompass the full range of moral regulations, since the moral behaviour of individuals is also governed through private, constitutional, and administrative law. These modern forms of legal regulation do not claim to distinguish right from wrong, but simply to define certain acts as legal or illegal. Nevertheless, various branches of law, from municipal by-laws to family law, criminal statutes, and immigration law, are meant to govern our *moral* conduct.

Most of us have thought about law's relationship to morality, even if we have not considered the changing history of that relationship. Laws, simply put, are rules and regulations determined by an authoritative body. Once laws are proclaimed, we abide by them, violate them, and change them in a variety of contexts, ranging from playgrounds to Parliament. Not surprisingly, laws that govern morality, like any laws, vary from jurisdiction to jurisdiction, and they change over time.

Morality is more difficult to define because it is an abstract concept. For our purposes here, it is a strategy of evaluation or a means of distinguishing between goodness and badness. Thus, notions of morality dictate behavioural ideals (one should act morally) and simultaneously condemn the failure to uphold those ideals (thereby defining *im*morality). Moralists are more likely than legislators to claim that their rules are absolute and unchanging. However, morality is no less contestable than law, as debates within and between religious factions confirm.

At first glance, secular laws may appear disconnected from morality. However, closer inspection reveals that these laws provide state-sanctioned muscle to enforce informal moral codes. Morality is certainly the province of parental guides and religious institutions, but law enforcement officers, courts, and correctional agents are officially empowered to issue orders and to enforce compliance. Parents may teach children that stealing is immoral, but criminal statutes define theft as a criminal act; moreover, according to the law, the consequences of criminal offences are not damnation or a scolding, but specified penalties, such as fines or imprisonment.

This legal power to back moral guidelines with the force of law explains why law is always a site of struggle, among those who seek to impose particular visions of morality, those who reject them, and those who propose alternatives.

Tracing which moral projects become legally sanctioned provides clues to help us identify the winners and losers in those struggles.

But what of 'regulation'? This, too, is a familiar term which requires definition if we are to conceptualize the relation between law and morality. Until recently, historians and social scientists favoured the term 'social control' to describe the state's power over citizens. The problem with that term was that it gave an impression of *total* control – depicting the state as a kind of hammer poised over the people. So where does that leave resistance? How can we analyse ineffective laws, or institutions that *fail* to control? Theorists influenced by philosopher Michel Foucault have urged scholars to abandon the social-control model for a more flexible concept of regulation. Many scholars have accordingly tossed away the image of the hammer in favour of that of the net – restrictive, yet full of holes.

Regulation theorists have also emphasized that state agencies and institutions are not the sole means by which behaviour is regulated. While the police, the courts, and the prisons are obviously in the business of regulating individuals, so, too, are other organizations, including religious institutions, schools, factories, families, peer groups, and even illegal groups, such as gangs. The rise of state agencies geared towards regulation was a critical factor in modern state formation, but they never supplanted these extra-legal regulatory agencies. Although this book addresses law as a means of moral regulation, we are keenly aware that we are treading on but one patch of a much wider field of study.

Finally, studying law on the books allows us to address regulatory objectives, but it reveals nothing about actual processes of moral regulation. And concentrating on formal law reinforces the false impression that legal statutes provide the only means of regulation. Thus, we are also concerned here with the laws in action. For instance, the production, distribution, and consumption of alcohol were severely restricted throughout much of Canada in the 1910s and early 1920s through a patchwork of federal, provincial, and municipal laws. However, we do not assume that those laws explain why alcohol consumption dropped (religious or health concerns may have provided more important motivation, for instance). And we certainly do not pretend that everyone obeyed the law! Here again the image of the net is instructive: at different times, and in different places, laws regulating morality were more or less restrictive. However, it has always been possible for individuals and groups to resist or evade legal regulations.

Defining Our Territory

In *Making Good* we chart connections between law and morality in early-national Canada by concentrating on the changing scope and subjects of regulation, the administration of morals laws, and the ideological interests which underlay the imposition of legislation. Before we proceed with the Canadian context, we introduce three key ideas that anchor our conceptualization of law's complex relationship with morality.

First, and foremost, we question the central tenet of liberal democracies – namely, that laws do not interfere with the enjoyment of life, except to curtail pleasures that may threaten the safety or security of others. This faith is based on idealized notions of the law *in theory*. Historical evidence confirms that the relation between law and morality *in practice* is neither so straightforward nor so benign. For one thing, the unprosecuted are likewise regulated, if only by the *threat* of enforcement. The compliant may internalize legal prescriptions in a bid to avoid legal sanctions, whereas deliberate violators often alter their behaviour to circumvent the law. Still others (marijuana 'smoke-in' participants come to mind) flagrantly flout laws to protest their validity or to urge reform. Law does not *create* morality, but merely sets boundaries that are inevitably overstepped. Still, morals laws influence *everyone's* behaviour, even though they are rarely enforced against more than small or definable minorities of violators.

Second, the alleged neutrality of morals laws is belied by their selective enforcement. The classic example is the common-law offence of vagrancy, a modern vestige of an ancient status offence. Not only is it elastic in definition (incorporating singing in the streets, living in a cart, and wandering highways or fields, among other sorts of behaviour), but it acquired different meanings, depending upon the objects of enforcement in different historical periods. Unemployed men in the nineteenth century could be rounded up under the pretext that they were 'tramps,' while young women suspected of prostitution could also be arrested for vagrancy if found unescorted on city streets at night. Invariably, the less powerful are vulnerable to sanctions imposed by those better able to invoke the coercive powers of the state.

Finally, we argue that looking for morals legislation exclusively under legally defined categories of morality (such as incest or birth control) restricts the scope for inquiry. The regulation of sexual morality is a major preoccupation of morals laws, but sexuality is only one aspect of morality. Defined as much through lifestyle and attitude as through overt acts, morality embraces a diverse set of expectations. Accordingly, rewards, as well as punishment, are often linked to tests of character. For instance, in the 1920s and 1930s it was not 'illegal' for single mothers to go out dancing or to entertain men, but they might find their allowances cut off if news of their 'immorality' reached granting authorities. Similar requirements were demanded of immigrants. Early immigration laws not only defined *who* could become a Canadian, but defined in *moral* terms who might be excluded from the benefits of Canadian citizenship.

Our analysis of law's connections to morality provokes further questions for our historical exploration: why did some moral notions, and not others, find expression in law? what accounts for the timing of moral regulations' initial appearance? how were laws enforced, and why were they sometimes ignored or broken? why were some sorts of people more or less likely to find themselves singled out as objects of moral regulation? which agencies, aside from the state, were able or eager to participate in the legal regulation of morality? Although such questions have puzzled philosophers and theorists for centuries, we will tackle them on more restricted turf: the history of Canada in the late nineteenth and early twentieth centuries.

Making Good

In this book, we look at the changing relationship between law and morality during a critical phase of nation-building, from Confederation to the onset of the Second World War. Over that period, numerous forms of law – municipal, civil, criminal, constitutional – evolved, and an expanding range of institutions and agencies emerged to put laws into effect. Specific laws targeted 'immorality,' but the sorts of activities deemed immoral, the means of monitoring immoral behaviour, and the types of sanctions imposed varied considerably over the nineteenth and twentieth centuries. Similarly, mechanisms of legal moral regulation varied between provinces, between cities and rural areas, and between French Catholic and Anglo-Celtic, and Protestant, Canada. However the overriding objective in early-national Canada was to build a great nation, not just with a transcontinental railway and stout farmers, but with citizens made good.

Making good citizens is a terribly tall order, as disappointed moral reformers privately admitted. Eradicating immorality is a noble aim, but it is unattainable, in part because definitions of morality constantly evolve. What is immoral in one period (for instance, gambling) may become a laudable industry in another (lotteries that channel money into charities, for example). So, even though Canada never acquired a reputation as a nation of rogues or ne'er-do-wells, neither did it turn into a country peopled by morally upright citizens. Despite the best efforts of moral campaigners and legal reformers, the ongoing project of moral regulation through law was always vulnerable to resistance, subversion, and non-compliance.

Through various branches of the emerging Canadian state, a loose network of laws regulated morality by proscribing unacceptable behaviour in every sphere of life, including the family, work, and leisure. Yet legally defined immorality in Canada was neither fixed nor uniformly applied. As countervailing pressures were exerted by those who complained that laws were too lax, and those who claimed that citizens ought to enjoy greater freedom to determine their own moral conduct, definitions of immorality were openly contested, and sometimes altered.

Some had more cause than others to complain about the invasiveness of the law. Legal moral regulation was in many respects a project of imposing upon aboriginals, the poor, immigrants, children, and women standards of conduct idealized (but often flouted) by the principal powerholders in early-national Canada: wealthy Anglo-Celtic Protestants and, to a lesser extent, bourgeois French Catholics. Examining the history of the legal enforcement of moral regulation inevitably exposes the broader patterns of unequal power relations in Canadian history.

Political leaders in the early-national period did not envision just any kind of nation, but one that would facilitate capital accumulation. Central to that goal was the heterosexual family comprising a male breadwinner and a wife dedicated to raising future productive Canadians. Any deviations that threatened the viability of the family – prostitution, homosexuality, abortion, equal employment opportunities for women – were major obsessions of morals regulators.

New citizens of good character were simultaneously sought from abroad and manufactured from within. When immigrants came to open up land for cultivation and to toil in industry, they were welcomed as compliant workers, not as labour agitators. When immigrants protested against their economic exploitation, or when they became victims of periodic economic downturns, they faced summary deportation, often on the pretext that they were unfit *moral* subjects. The acceptance of capitalist values was also a quality officially demanded of Native peoples. Under the Indian Act, aboriginals were required to take up sedentary farming, and to espouse economic individualism, in order to earn political enfranchisement. Evidence of minor moral lapses was sufficient to brand them as 'bad Indians.' Definitions of good character and habits of industry were virtually synonymous with the demands of the emergent Canadian capitalist order. Through a variety of legal means, including immigration laws, the Indian Act, vagrancy laws, and sedition statutes, those demands were backed by the powers of the state.

While the expanding national government was a powerful tool for the enforcement of gender-, class-, and racially encoded moral agendas, much was lost or scrambled in the translation. Powerful lobbyists certainly influenced the tenor and tenacity of legal moral regulation, but once morals laws were passed, their enforcement was not guaranteed. For one thing, the application of laws governing morality required resources, from jail cells to theatre censors' salaries, which tight-fisted administrators hated to waste. For another thing, the multiplication of laws regulating morality developed in an uncoordinated fashion. Inconsistency often bred conflicts when governance of individual municipalities and provinces differed. For instance, authorities in 'dry' areas found it impossible to control illegal drinking when citizens could travel to 'wet' areas for supplies.

Contradictions within morals regulation also arose when the application of laws produced unintended consequences. Over the late nineteenth and early twentieth centuries, a host of sexual offences became illegal for the first time, and many older ones were redefined in an attempt to protect people considered to be most vulnerable: youth and women, in particular. But many of these new laws proved difficult to enforce, and others ended up stigmatizing victims and exposing them to therapeutic intervention. Other ironies arose from the conflicts between racist and capitalist objectives underlying regulatory schemes. For instance, the federal government tried to 'civilize' Native people by forcing them to farm for profit; because European settlers resented aboriginal successes, they pressured Indian agents to scuttle their projects. Similarly, the state responded to many labour calls that non-British immigration be restricted to reduce competition, largely because anti-immigrant sentiment was widely shared at all levels of Canadian society.

In sum, writing a history of law and morals regulation is more than a matter of recounting all the laws which formally defined and explicitly prohibited immoral acts. By focusing on the law in action, and not only in theory, and by looking at morals regulation through laws apparently unrelated to morality, the picture grows more complicated and more intriguing.

Our exploration starts in 1867 and finishes in 1939, two dates which mark the beginning and the end of the early-national period. Over three-quarters of a century, Canada grew quickly from a cluster of colonies into a huge transcontinental nation. Determining precise moments when one phase of regulation transformed into another is somewhat artificial. None the less, we divide our survey into three broad periods during which significant transitions occurred in either the goals or the agencies of regulation. Part I, 'Framing the Nation,' deals with the period from Confederation to the election of Laurier's Liberals in 1896. It examines the introduction of formal legal structures of moral regulation. Part II, 'Envisioning Morality,' which covers 1896 to 1919, is concerned with the deepening commitment of the state to put religiously inspired moral reforms into legal form. Part III, 'Widening the Net,' looks at the interwar period, when the means and scope of moral regulation expanded, particularly through the suppression of radicalism and the rise of social welfare.

PART I: FRAMING THE NATION, 1867–1896

1

Building the Moral Dominion

Along the wide Border was no law or order,
The redman debased by the bootlegger's sway.
Unprincipled trader and 'Fort Whoop-up raider,'
The Montana 'Long-knives' were lords of the day.

'Mid orgies and mysteries, there were wailings and miseries;
Bloodlust and hatred were thereby revived.
But, at this crucial moment, with chaos in foment,
Commissioner French and his Mounties arrived.

George E. White, 'A Ballad of the West' (1940)

And things were forever changed. With the successful conclusion of their 1,000-mile trek in 1874, an event that became known as the 'Great March,' the newly formed
Mounties secured the West for Canada, despite the imperialistic designs of the United States, thus ensuring that the
young dominion would stretch from sea to sea. For many
Canadians, these geographic gains paled in significance
compared with the moral victory represented by the Great
March. When the Mounties raised the red ensign at Fort
Whoop-Up, they not only established Canadian sovereignty
in the West, but also guaranteed that a distinct kind of
order would prevail there, one that reflected the order
embodied by the Mounties themselves and that set the
dominion apart from the republic to the south. It was

characterized by centralized power, hierarchy, discipline, and a belief that the needs of the group came before those of the individual. In essence, the force embodied the 'peace, order, and good government' promised by the British North America Act.

Nowhere was the moral superiority of Canada's political order more apparent than in the character of the Mounties' authority. The force established order, not with guns ablazing, but through moral suasion. According to one observer, the phrase '"In the Queen's name," out of the mouth of an unarmed redcoat, with one hand lightly on your shoulder, carrie[d] more weight than a smoking gun.' Even the Americans recognized that the Mounties' power was different, particularly when it came to dealing with aboriginal peoples. One famous story had three Mounties relieve an entire column of the American cavalry who were escorting a band of allegedly bloodthirsty Indians out of U.S. territory: 'Where's your escort for these Indians?' the American commanding officer asked the Mountie. 'We're here, Colonel,' answered the Canadian corporal, referring to his modest complement of men.

The success of the Mounties in Canadianizing the West without the degree of bloodshed that characterized the American experience has produced the impression that the Canadian state was the pre-eminent moral agent in the early-national period. The argument put forward in this chapter is that such was not the case. (We leave it to next chapter to see whether or not the Mounties lived up to their reputation.) While the federal state was concerned with making a moral dominion, neither it nor the provinces dominated the apparatus of moral regulation from 1867 to 1896. Instead, moral regulation was accomplished by three different sets of lead actors: the federal and provincial states, the Roman Catholic and Protestant churches, and the local communities. In this chapter we survey the regulatory landscape, exploring the role of each of these moral agents in turn, making the point that each acted relatively independently from the others, and that the strength and importance of each depended on the regional context of regulation, and on who or what was being regulated.

The State of Affairs

John A. Macdonald had a far-sighted vision of Canada and took steps to realize it soon after Confederation. His 'National Policy' was aimed at ensuring the young dominion's greatness by laying the groundwork for economic prosperity through high tariffs, immigration and western settlement, and a transcontinental railway.

Yet, without the proper moral foundation, the young dominion would surely falter. Macdonald saw Confederation as a fundamentally moral act creating a virtuous, if small, nation. The original four provinces of Ontario, Quebec, Nova Scotia, and New Brunswick, joined later by Manitoba (1870), British Columbia (1871), and Prince Edward Island (1873), comprised a bulwark of British values in the face of the aggressive American republic. What the new Dominion of Canada lacked in size, it hoped to make up with the power it accorded the federal government. However, as we will see throughout this book, creating a moral dominion required a strong central government, yet it was also premised on a belief in individualism (as opposed to collective identities); hierarchical social relations; capitalist economics; and self-discipline, whether that came in the form of going to church, working hard, or simply resisting the sins of the flesh or the bottle. Above all, the foundation of the moral dominion rested on a belief in the traditional family and the ideology of separate spheres for men and women that underlay it.

The centrality of the family in a moral dominion was revealed in nervous discussions of divorce prior to the passage of the British North America Act. Fearful that a Protestant-dominated House of Commons would introduce divorce, French-Canadian delegates argued that the provinces should retain control over the matter. In response, federalists countered by pointing out that it would actually be harder for those who wanted a divorce law to get one passed at the federal level. Allowing the federal government to have jurisdiction over divorce would thus better ensure the sanctity of marriage. In any case, since marriage and family life were the bedrock of a moral dominion, retaining control over divorce was almost a matter of national security – and, like all such matters, belonged in the jurisdiction of the federal government. It was a convincing argument, and when the British North America Act was passed, Parliament retained the right to legislate in matters of divorce and marriage. As Constance Backhouse argues, Canada's stance on divorce became a matter of self-congratulation and a source of national distinctiveness, particularly in contrast with the United States. In 1867, the editors of one of the nation's law journals argued that the liberal American divorce laws were proving 'ruinous' to 'the morals, well-being and the entire social interests of communities ...'

The federal government also retained the sole power to legislate in the area of criminal law. Certain activities remained offences at common law, and pre-existing colonial criminal statutes remained in force, but the BNA Act conferred on Ottawa the power to create any new criminal legislation. The federal government also took on the project of prescribing punishment for those convicted of serious criminal offences.

However, as federal legislators would discover, there was a gap – and occasionally a chasm – between law and its enforcement, the latter being under provincial jurisdiction. As we will see throughout this book, the courts and the police did not always act in accordance with the wishes of the federal government. They had their own agendas for moral regulation, and were subjected to a variety of local pressures that complicated law enforcement, making it uneven across time and place.

In the early-national period, the federal state was in fact a relatively weak moral agent, reacting to bad behaviour after it occurred, rather than trying to shape the conduct and values of its citizens to prevent moral breaches. It relied primarily on the criminal law to impose morality. Contrary to what we might expect, relatively few acts were immoral according to the law. Murder, rape, theft, and drunk and disorderly behaviour were, of course, defined as criminal offences in 1867, but there were few legal strictures on sexual conduct or provisions for the protection of girls and women. For instance, procuring was not a criminal offence in the early-national period, nor was seduction. Sodomy was, but the offence of 'gross indecency,' the primary weapon against homosexuality, did not exist until 1890. Moreover, the lesser offences of attempted rape and indecent assault, which would later account for many sexual-assault convictions, had not yet been formally added to federal criminal statutes.

The criminal law could deal with criminal behaviour, such as homicide, assault, or theft, but proved to be a fairly blunt and ineffective tool for regulating activities that were less clearly either right or wrong. The criminalization of trade-union activity is a good example. At common law, 'combinations' of workers who collaborated in order to drive up wages were deemed 'criminal conspiracies.' Not only did employers consider them offensive because they breached the old paternal relationship that had governed master-and-servant dealings for generations, but they also believed that these combinations were threats to peace and prosperity: workers who withdrew their labour in the hopes of raising their wages often resorted to intimidation and violence to keep other workers from taking their jobs.

Despite the clarity of the law against combinations, and the antipathy of many employers towards trade unions, few workers were actually prosecuted for criminal conspiracy in the nineteenth century. Employers had to acknowledge the public's growing toleration for workers' combinations or face the prospect of uncertain convictions. Given the growing concentration of capital in the 1850s and 1860s, the power disparities between employer and employee seemed unreasonable, particularly by the early 1870s, when the courts ruled that combinations of employers, like the Canadian Manufacturers' Association, were legal as long as they did not unduly 'restrain' trade. Continuing to single out unions for prosecution would be an obvious affront to the idea of formal equality before the law, and threatened to undermine its legitimacy altogether. In the 1872 Trade Union Act, the federal government finally legalized such organizations. Thereafter, it sought to regulate unions indirectly, though no less effectively.

Legislators were unprepared to jettison the criminal law, however unwieldy its nature. Instead, they hoped to make it more effective. At Confederation, the Dominion government had to rationalize the criminal laws of four separate colonial jurisdictions, each of which had received a different body of English law when it had been declared a colony. The problem only got worse as new provinces entered Confederation. The solution was to codify the criminal law of Canada, to reduce it to a single body, with offences organized by type. For Macdonald, codification was a project in nation-building, akin to building the Canadian Pacific Railway; like the railway, a criminal code would unite disparate jurisdictions. Canada's new criminal code of 1892 was the first codification in the Empire, and a model for other nations. Although codification facilitated criminal prosecutions, as its supporters contended, greater clarity in the law also meant that it would become more easily contested and politicized by moral reformers – as we will see in Part II.

At the same time, federal legislators attempted to make certain bodies of law more effective, especially those relating to sexual activity and the protection of girls and women. The late nineteenth century stands out for its legislative activity in this area. The impetus for change came, not from the Department of Justice, but from one very energetic man, David Watt, and his Montreal Society for the Protection of Girls and Women. Watt and his group inundated the department with draft bills, petitions, and pamphlets with such titles as *Immoral Legislation*, urging Ottawa to save innocent girls and women from the clutches of evil procurers and procuresses determined to consign them to a life of prostitution. In response to such pressure, and in line with British precedent, Ottawa passed a series of laws from 1869 to 1892 aimed at preventing the 'debauchery' of young women. Everything, it seemed, short of the sale of sex for money was made a criminal offence or punished more severely than previously.

Watt and other moral reformers also convinced Parliament to criminalize seduction in 1886. Over the next several years, the legal definition of seduction law was embellished through a series of amendments. Technically, the crime of seduction covered all heterosexual liaisons in which: a girl or woman was under age fourteen (later sixteen); a woman under twenty-one was made a promise of marriage; or a woman under twenty-one had sex with her guardian or employer. In all cases, the female had to be of 'previously chaste character' to be considered a victim. In effect, seduction law legally defined what most Canadians believed: good girls could be seduced; bad girls could not.

The law dealing with coercive sex – rape – also changed. In general, rape shifted from being a crime against male property (in this case, the reproductive capacity of a man's wife or daughter) to become a crime against the person. It was thus no longer necessary to prove penetration. In addition, recognizing the difficulties in securing convictions for rape, Ottawa made provision in 1874 for alternative sentences to be applied to those convicted of the crime (rape remained a capital offence, but judges could now substitute terms of imprisonment). At the same time, the Criminal Code was amended to define the lesser crimes of assault with intent to rape, and indecent assault. According to Graham Parker, by the end of the nineteenth century these

changes in the laws relating to sexual activity and the protection of girls and women were the most comprehensive in
the Empire.

Yet all the law in the world was of no use if it was not enforced. Law enforcement lay strictly within the purview of
the provinces with one exception – the North-West Territories, which, as Canada's colony, were under federal jurisdiction. Though the Deed of Surrender transferring the region
from the Hudson's Bay Company to the Dominion was final-
ized in 1869, the Riel Rebellion proved just how tenuous
Canada's hold over the Northwest was. The Métis were paci-
fied for the time being, but American whisky traders could
create even greater trouble. Liquor had been a catalyst for
many of the bloody Indian wars that had come to character-
ize the American frontier, and Macdonald did not want the
same events repeated in Canadian territory. If nothing else,
sustained warfare would bankrupt the young dominion and
deter prospective immigrants – and western settlement was
crucial to if Canada were to grow and prosper.

Enter the North-West Mounted Police (NWMP) as the
instrument of central Canadian imperialism. Established in
1873, the force, then 300 strong, marched west the next
year. According to S.W. Horrall, in the first decade of
its operation, the NWMP largely succeeded in carrying
out its mandate: it put a serious crimp in the liquor trade
and acted as a buffer between aboriginals and a less-than-
sympathetic Euro-Canadian population, as well as some
overly zealous officials in the Department of Indian Affairs.

The Mounties also considered it their task to assimilate
newly arrived immigrants. In his 1893 report, the NWMP's
Commissioner Herchmer underlined the importance of
'laying a good moral foundation at the start through the
activity and vigilance of the police.' 'The opinion these
people [the immigrants] form of our administration of the
laws on their first arrival has the greatest possible effect on
their future conduct,' he noted. 'An inability on our part to
impress them with the necessity of strictly obeying our laws,

will,' he argued, 'be certain to lead to heavy expenses later on in the administration of justice.' R.C. Macleod has shown that the Mounties considered their patrols and visits as opportunities to explain the law to newly arrived settlers and to impress upon them the importance of obedience. No one escaped these lessons: from Germans and Ukrainians, to Americans and British settlers, all were schooled in the Canadian way. This assimilationist project was accomplished with remarkably little resistance, and relied on a relatively small force: 500 in 1882, 1,000 in 1885 (the year of the rebellion), and 750 by the end of the century. Thus a legend was born.

Once the Mounties, or any other police force, got their man, what did the state do with him? People convicted of serious crimes – that is, those meriting a sentence of two years plus a day or more – were sent to federally administered penitentiaries to serve their terms. The penitentiaries built in Kingston in 1835, in Saint John in 1841, and in Halifax in 1844, all became federal institutions after Confederation, along with St Vincent de Paul, opened in Quebec in 1873; Stony Mountain, in Manitoba in 1874; Oakalla, in British Columbia in 1878; and Dorchester, in New Brunswick in 1880 (which replaced those in Halifax and Saint John).

The roots of the penitentiary stretched back a century. It was born out of the convergence of two streams of late-eighteenth-century English reform thought and activity: one evangelical and the other utilitarian. From the evangelical stream came a belief that criminals, like all sinners, could be saved, and that penal institutions should reform, not just punish, wrongdoers. Utilitarian reformers promoted the idea that the criminal law would deter crime more effectively if the punishment meted out to offenders was proportional to the severity of their crimes. The death penalty would be retained, but only for the most serious crimes. All other offences would merit terms of imprisonment. Changing the pattern of sentencing in this way, however, brought an increase in the prison population.

The penitentiary thus emerged in the early nineteenth century as a means to achieve two goals: reformation of criminals, and deterrence of crime. The inner workings of early penitentiaries bore the imprint of evangelicalism and were aimed at nothing less than the complete transformation of the criminal's character. Inmates were first stripped of their identities (their hair was closely cropped, they wore uniforms, and they were identified by numbers), and then subjected to a regime of work and religious reflection, both of which were carried out in strict silence and designed to make them anew. The path to reform lay in reading the Bible in their cells and working at any number of jobs, from completing the penitentiary at Kingston to manufacturing shoes and brooms at Saint John. This program reflected the belief that people fell into a life of crime because they lacked the self-discipline that governed those who had learned to labour properly and who had internalized the biblical injunctions against temptation.

Canadian penitentiaries never actually fulfilled their mandate of disciplining convicts to become industrious Christian workers, however. Penitentiary supporters' expectations proved to be unrealistic. The public resisted prison labour because it was unfair competition. The institutions were overcrowded and underfunded. It was difficult to administer the penitentiary program as it had been envisioned, particularly the rule of silence. Getting prisoners to comply with the host of other rules governing their conduct on the inside became an end in itself. As the 1849 Brown Commission, struck to investigate the administration of Kingston Penitentiary, discovered, the warden and guards spent most of their time flogging convicts for infractions of the rules. Envisioned first as a radical experiment in reform, the penitentiary ended up being a new way to punish.

The penitentiaries stand out as agents of moral regulation because of their self-conscious attempt to reform inmates' characters, but they were consistent with the generally reactive state policy of dealing with bad behaviour after it happened rather than trying to prevent it in the first place. The exception was the state's regulation of Canada's First Nations. Soon after Confederation, aboriginal peoples were deemed to be the only Canadians who required an entire bureaucracy with statutory authority. Under the British North America Act, the federal government received full jurisdiction over Native peoples, dealing with them, first, through the Secretary of State; then, through the Department of the Interior, and, finally, through the Department of Indian Affairs (1880). The first consolidated Indian Act (1876) defined who an Indian was, deemed such persons wards of the state, and then singled them out for special treatment. Being a 'status Indian' became, in an informal sense, a 'status offence' – that is, a crime defined, not by a particular action (by someone *doing* something like robbing or murdering or raping), but by the individual's identity. Thus, the Indian Act offers a prime example of how regulation can create problems or offences that then justify state action.

The Indian Act and the Department of Indian Affairs (DIA) were unabashedly concerned with transforming the character of all aboriginals, by protecting, civilizing, and assimilating the 'savages' to Anglo-Canadian norms. In the mid-nineteenth century, many people believed the First Nations were a 'vanishing race,' an endangered species that had to be protected on 'reserves,' where they would not fall prey to big-city temptations and unscrupulous whites. Once they were protected on the reserves, the process of civilization could begin, as John Tobias has argued. Aboriginals were broken of their 'nomadic' habits and taught to 'improve' their land in the European style. Instead of going off to hunt or fish, they were expected to stay on the land, farming it to subsist. If they kept their farms up, and could prove themselves of good moral character and not in debt (qualifications that many Euro-Canadian settlers would have had a hard time meeting), they were given title to their parcel of reserve land, and the right to vote. At that point, they were also deemed to be fully assimilated, and hence they ceased to be 'Indians' under the definition of the act, becoming, instead, full Canadian citizens. The idea was that, as more and more Indians were enfranchised in this way, reserves would disappear, as would the Indian problem.

The DIA believed that the best chances for lasting results would be achieved with First Nations children. The federal government had always supported the missionaries in their long-standing attempts to educate the First Nations, but in 1879 they decided to take a more direct and active role in education by setting up their own residential schools, where children could be assimilated far from the allegedly corrupting environment of their homes and families. In Canada, residential education took two main forms in the period under study: small boarding-schools for young children, and larger 'industrial schools' for older students. The first industrial schools were established in 1883, funded by Ottawa and the Christian churches, and administered by individual clergymen or nuns. By 1890 there were fourteen such schools, and by 1900 twenty-two. The majority were in British Columbia, the Prairies, and the Far North, where the stiff competition for souls among various Christian orders manifested itself in a flurry of school-building. With the odd exception, such as the residential school at Shubenacadie, few institutions of this sort were erected east of Ontario.

Like the penitentiary, the industrial school was meant to be a total institution, combining religious teaching and work, both intended to instil Christian and bourgeois habits and values. On enrolling, aboriginal boys had their hair closely cropped, and both they and the girls were washed and given uniforms. In a typical school, boys were put through a five-year program designed to give them a trade and to teach them how to read, write, and pray. In their final two years, they spent all their time in on-site workshops as full-time apprentices in carpentry, tinsmithing, printing, boot-making, and tailoring. Girls were taught to cook, sew, clean, and do laundry. Until they completed the cycle of civilization by marrying a boy from a residential school, these skills would make them employable as domestics.

The industrial-school regime also facilitated assimilation by limiting parental visits and students' trips home and by insisting, on pain of punishment, that only English be spoken. Like all students (or prisoners, for that matter), Native pupils were marched through a fairly rigorous schedule of activities – to the sound of a bell – meant to socialize them to the kind of discipline they would meet in the workplace. Even their leisure time was managed to ensure that students engaged only in rational recreation – playing baseball and cricket, or performing British patriotic songs in the school brass band.

Policing and Punishment

The various provincial states also involved themselves in policing and punishment, taking a more-or-less reactive stance, with the important exception of education. In the absence of any national authority, differences between provinces arose, as did disparities within them, particularly between urban and rural areas.

Policing was a prime example of the unevenness of moral regulation in the second half of the nineteenth century. Though Canada's largest cities – Toronto, Montreal, Quebec, Saint John, Halifax, and Charlottetown – all had forces before Confederation, rural residents (who comprised about 85 per cent of the population in 1867) had only a justice of the peace to turn to if they found themselves the victims of crime. Though the number of municipal police forces grew in the second half of the nineteenth century, most were small: for instance, the one in Amherst, Nova Scotia, established in the late 1880s, employed only two constables. Most forces grew out of the old volunteer night watch, and were not staffed by professionally trained men.

Constables responded to crime rather than trying to prevent it, and had little time to investigate individual cases.

For the most part, municipal forces imposed morality by policing a variety of public-order offences, hauling mainly working-class people in for drunk-and-disorderly behaviour, lewdness, and vagrancy. Occasionally, as in Saint John, constables also found themselves policing strikes, guaranteeing 'free labour' by protecting replacement workers, and making sure picket-line scuffles did not escalate into more serious altercations. After 1878 and the passage of the Canada Temperance Act (Scott Act), constables in the cities and towns, in Atlantic Canada especially, found themselves charged with the unenviable task of making sure the establishments on their beats remained dry. Pressed by the city's moral reformers to clean up Saint John's 'dance halls, gin hovels, and dens of perdition,' the police came into greater contact and conflict with the working class.

Because of the role the municipal police played in enforcing public order, some historians have argued that municipal officers acted as 'domestic missionaries,' imposing bourgeois ideals of respectable behaviour on the working class, just as those who ministered to the Indians tried to get their charges to embrace the norms of 'civility.' As Greg Marquis points out, the process was a contested one, and many considered the police and the magistrates' courts to be nothing more than 'a machine of oppression under the guise of law.' The working class were certainly the prime targets of policing. In the last third of the nineteenth century, specialized institutions emerged at the provincial level to reform these working-class criminals by instilling in them proper work habits as well as particular skills. Here, Ontario proved to be the leader in corrections, as in all things moral.

The construction of the Andrew Mercer Ontario Reformatory for Females in 1874 reflected the prevailing belief that women were different, and needed a different kind of moral reformation. Whereas Ontario's Central Prison, opened in 1874 for men, was designed to be a 'terror to evil-doers,' the Mercer was envisioned as a prison 'governed by kindness.' Overseen by a 'matron' who combined motherly love and discipline, the Mercer was to be run as 'an ordinary, well-conducted household,' where the inmates would be rehabilitated through work and learn to 'support themselves by honest labour when [they were] restored to liberty.' But, whereas men at the Central Prison were put to work manufacturing railway cars, the Mercer's women were subjected to lessons in remedial domesticity. They were taught how to cook, sew, and do laundry – tasks that befitted their gender and class, and that would not only discipline them, but also prepare them for paid work in domestic service, or unpaid work in marriage.

Correctional institutions for boys and girls were also built on the premise that they, too, were different, both from each other and from adults. One could not hope to reform wayward children and save them from a life of crime if they were housed with hardened adult criminals. Ontario, as usual, led the way, establishing the Penetanguishene Reformatory for Boys in 1861, locating it (as were Indian reserves) far from the corrupting influence of cities.

Ontario's 'child-savers' soon concluded that many children housed at reformatories were simply 'neglected' by their working-class parents, and that their moral education was not well served by mixing them with children who were truly delinquent. Industrial schools, modelled on European reform schools and houses of refuge, emerged in Ontario in the 1880s to discipline these working-class 'savages' to bourgeois notions of civility. The family again provided the rehabilitative model. Paul Bennett notes that, at the Victoria Industrial School for Boys, for instance, pupils were housed in 'cottages,' each with a 'mother' and a 'father,' otherwise known as a 'matron' and a 'guard'.

The same concern for discipline and moral development that animated these correctional institutions also undergirded the public schools. The state-funded, secular, and universal system of public schooling was something relatively new at Confederation. Ontario had again set the pace. Egerton Ryerson and other school promoters in the 1840s and 1850s had argued that state education would ensure that children internalized appropriate political attitudes. Loyalty to the British Crown and a respect for hierarchy and authority were considered the pillars of citizenship and good character, as Bruce Curtis argues. Reformers were particularly concerned with imposing school discipline on the children of the working class. If nothing was done about the 'waifs and strays' on Toronto's streets, reformers believed, they would certainly grow up to be the criminal class of the future. The newspaper reports pointing to the growing numbers of 'street *arabs*' suggest that reformers pictured children of the poor to be a race apart – children whose 'viciousness' made them little different from the 'savages' on reserves and in Native industrial schools.

As a result of these concerns, a system of state-funded, secular schooling was in place in Ontario by Confederation, and was completed in 1871, with the passage of the first compulsory schools act. Though the Ryerson model was replicated in other provinces in the late nineteenth century, there was one exception: Quebec.

Religion and Regulation

In the 1840s, the Roman Catholic Church (and not the state) managed to position itself as the prime defender of French-Canadian identity. Like Ontario's school promoters, Canada East's conservative and nationalist clergy believed that education was crucial to building character and making citizens. However, their success came in the establishment of denominationally based schools run by separate and independent Roman Catholic and Protestant boards. At Confederation, Quebec retained this dual school system, and the School Act of 1875 effectively eliminated any significant state control in that sphere until the Quiet Revolution in the 1950s.

The church had to remain ever vigilant, as events in

Manitoba proved. There, in 1890, the province's Liberal government abolished public funding for Catholic schools, despite the fact that the Manitoba Act of 1870 had formally established a dual system of education. According to D'Alton McCarthy, a prominent anti-Catholic politician, giving special status to the French language and allowing denominational schools to exist in Manitoba violated the principle of separation of church and state; furthermore, it threatened the social order because it perpetuated sectarianism. If separate schools were not dismantled, the young dominion would inevitably founder. Though McCarthy did not consider himself or his recommendations to be anti-French, French Canadians had reason to fear assimilation. 'Where we have so many different nationalities, it is necessary,' the *Gladstone Age* argued, 'to bind them together and blend their characteristics into one common nationality.' Though Prime Minister Wilfrid Laurier convinced the province to withdraw the bill, separate schools were not reinstated. French was placed on a status equal to (and as low as) other non-English languages, contrary to the notion of a biracial nation entrenched in the British North America Act.

Education was only one field in which organized religion played a prominent role in regulating morality. Apart from doling out advice in sermons, Sunday-school classes, and philanthropic work with the poor and needy, both Catholic and Protestant churches also wielded considerable indirect influence over public manners and morals through a variety of religious lay organizations. In the nineteenth century the most important were those devoted to moderating or eliminating alcohol consumption.

Temperance was one of the most important moral-reform movements of the nineteenth century, in terms of both the number of adherents and its effects. In the first half of the century, the movement was deeply coloured by Protestant evangelicalism, particularly in Atlantic Canada, where it had originated and enjoyed its first legislative successes. Salvation could come only to those who eschewed the pleasures of 'demon rum,' as passionate speakers exhorted crowds of onlookers at temperance gatherings. In Quebec, as Jan Noel argues, temperance advocacy and nationalism were linked: if French Canadians rejected the bottle, Roman Catholic temperance advocates argued, they would be able to compete more successfully with the powerful anglophone minority, and eventually reclaim their rightful share of political and economic power. After 1850, however, the movement conveyed a more complicated message: temperance became a marker of respectability for both the middle class and the respectable working class in an industrial age which placed a greater value on efficiency and sobriety.

While some Canadians were drawn to the movement out of their concern for workforce productivity, many more were moved by the gruesome tales of how alcohol destroyed home life – graphic stories of men who left the tavern broke but 'pretty full,' arriving at home only to beat their wives and children. As a result, temperance became a cause particularly dear to women, and especially to Anglo-Canadian middle-class women, who, in 1874, formed the Woman's Christian Temperance Union (WCTU). By 1883, the association went national, and by 1900 boasted 10,000 members. Through petitioning and education, the WCTU managed to convince the federal government to pass the Canada Temperance Act (the Scott Act) in 1878, allowing each municipality to decide through a plebiscite whether it would be 'wet' or 'dry.'

Though alcohol affected everyone who indulged, in practice temperance amounted to a campaign to change the habits of 'rough' (as opposed to 'respectable') working-class men. Middle- or upper-class men who drank in hotels or at home, and then abused their families, escaped censure, even though they indulged in a similar vice. In practice, then, the war against alcohol was not fought on all fronts, but was limited to the rougher elements of the working class. In Montreal, for instance, reform groups like the Young Men's Christian Association (YMCA), the Montreal Citizens' League, and the Society for the Prevention of Cruelty to Animals lobbied to close taverns like Joe Beef's. Joe's, an institution on the city's waterfront, also provided food, shelter, and medical assistance to working-class patrons, and doubled as a hiring hall for longshoreman. But to temperance reformers it was only a dissolute tavern that had to be closed, and its customers directed to more rational and respectable recreations.

'Rough Justice': Community-Based Moral Regulation

Shutting down taverns like Joe's and enforcing the Scott Act were not easy or always successful. Working-class communities, and, in particular, working-class men, had their own ideas about what was moral. On occasion, their resistance to do-gooders who tried to impose their own notions of right and wrong on them could turn violent. In Georgetown, Ontario, for instance, the Salvation Army's campaign to reform the rough habits of the town's working-class men was answered by a white-capping: harassment by local men disguised in masks, hoods, and robes. In Montreal in 1885, the Sanitary Police as well as the city's regular constables were attacked by working-class francophones when they tried to enforce the city's compulsory-vaccination by-law. As Lynne Marks details, those who dared to testify against their local publican might have their houses broken into and be beaten, as happened in Ingersoll. In Woodstock, two men who appeared as witnesses in a Scott Act case were attacked by a crowd of 200 'rowdies.' Such resistance was not confined to Euro-Canadians. When British Columbia lumbermill owner Sewell Moody confronted his Native employees for drinking whisky and then not showing up for work, in the 1870s, they stripped him naked and marched him from their reserve to the sawmill, the Roman Catholic priests trailing the procession, carrying the boss's clothes.

While enforcing community norms could be as simple

and direct as a punch in the nose, Thomas Stone's work on the miners' meeting and Allan Greer's and Bryan Palmer's work on the charivari demonstrate that communal forms of regulation could also be complex and subtle, involving the creation of parallel structures of authority. The miners' meeting offers one example. A form of local government, it emerged on the gold fields of British Columbia in the late 1850s and in the Yukon in the 1890s, before formal legal institutions were established there. Miners who worked a particular stretch of creek would convene to resolve disputes by a simple majority vote. They dealt with conflicting claims and water rights, but they also passed rules regarding liquor consumption and the propriety of relationships with aboriginal women, meting out punishment to those who transgressed them.

The charivari, an aggressive ritual rooted in plebeian culture, was another form of community-based moral regulation. Its origins lay in medieval Europe, where it governed marriage, preventing 'mismatches,' or unions in which the couple's motives were suspect. People who married too soon after being widowed, who married someone significantly younger or older, or who married for lust or money could find themselves targeted. Though local clergymen did their best to ferret out those who harboured bad intentions, discerning the motives of marrying couples was a difficult, if not impossible, task. In any case, actually preventing marriages from occurring was not something that clergy, themselves members of the community, could do (at least not on a regular basis) without compromising their own authority and that of the institution they represented. Suspicions, however well founded, would have had to remain just that, were it not for the charivari.

As an expression of popular sentiment, rather than a formal edict imposed from on high, the charivari allowed villagers to act on their suspicions, sending out clear messages about standards of propriety while not risking irreparable damage to social relations and cohesion. Once identified, the deviant couple was subjected to an unannounced nocturnal visit from the charivari crowd, a group consisting of members of the community (both men and women) who wore costumes or blackened their faces to disguise their identities. Once gathered outside the deviants' house, the crowd serenaded the couple with pots and pans, horns, whistles, and catcalls. The point was to get the couple to come out and 'face the music.' Once rousted up, the couple could be made to undergo some sort of ritual debasement before the community, such as being made to ride a donkey backwards while naked. Once humiliated, the offending couple was expected to pay a charivari 'fine' for their transgressions – a penalty which mirrored formal legal sanctions. After the penalty was exacted, the harassment ended, and life for all returned to its usual pattern.

Although the charivari's targets diversified over time, and it came to be practised by Catholics and Protestants, its form (the noisy nocturnal visits) remained the same. Couples who had made inappropriate marriages remained vulnerable, but so also were those who transgressed the norms of sexual propriety, were socially pretentious, violated the unspoken rules that governed the paternal relations between employer and employee, or made unpopular political decisions. Well into the twentieth century, such transgressors found themselves targeted. Thus, the charivari evolved into a means of regulating public as well as private behaviour.

As the history of the charivari indicates, community-based modes of moral regulation bore similarities to legal means of governing morality. In fact, moral regulations which were formalized over the late nineteenth and early twentieth centuries were in some respects derivative. For instance, charivaris were publicly condemned, but the ritual communicated and enforced moral values subsequently expressed in statute law. Similarly, though the rough justice of the miners' meetings was criticized, the formal legal institutions introduced in both British Columbia and the

Yukon were to a great extent patterned on them: B.C.'s Gold Commissioner's Court was advised by a panel of miners to ensure local input, and the Mounties stationed in the Yukon punished offenders in ways similar to those adopted at the miners' meetings.

Conclusion

Though John A. Macdonald and the fathers of Confederation envisioned Canada as a moral dominion and put a strong central government in place to achieve and maintain that vision, the apparatus of moral regulation in the early-national period was not dominated by either the federal or the provincial states. Instead, Roman Catholic and Protestant churches and local communities exercised considerable power in trying making people good. They did so largely unencumbered and undisturbed by the state, whose interest in moral regulation was restricted to a concern with criminal law, policing, and incarceration.

The division of powers enumerated in the British North America Act meant that moral regulation would vary regionally, and, in this respect, Quebec stood out. There, the Roman Catholic Church loomed especially large in making citizens good through its role in education. There were also differences between urban and rural areas, particularly in the form and character of policing. But equally significantly, there were differences in the targets of moral regulation. Despite its otherwise reactive stance, the federal government intervened directly and aggressively in the lives of Canada's First Nations, bent on transforming their manners and morals completely, making so-called savages into Canadian citizens. To a lesser extent, non-Native children, women, working-class men, and immigrants, all found themselves the objects of regulatory schemes launched by a variety of moral agents. Since virtue was seen to be distributed unevenly, the efforts at making good had to be as well.

2

Instituting Morality

The Mounties' Great March West little resembled the mythology it spawned. In fact, it was nothing short of disastrous: they got lost and rained on, ran out of water, were attacked by grasshoppers and mosquitoes, and came down with dysentery so severe that they retched in their saddles. To add insult to injury, when they finally found Fort Whoop-Up, lair of the evil American whisky traders, it was deserted. The contrast between myth and reality reminds us that the law on the books is often very different from the law in action. Legal regulations might be framed to achieve certain high-minded ends, but their enforcement can be problematic, and the consequences unexpected, or even contradictory. In some cases, the regulatory cure turned out to be worse than the moral disease. In this chapter we explore the differences between the intended effects of moral regulation and its actual results.

'The Red Serge of Courage'

Nowhere were the linkages between nation-building and character-building more apparent than in the West. Establishing dominion over the region involved laying down values as well as survey lines. It meant establishing order and respect for hierarchy and centralized authority, as well as eliminating the kind of violence that characterized the American frontier.

There to oversee the incorporation of the West and to enforce those values were Canada's men in scarlet. Showing the flag was only one of the force's many duties, and not its most pressing one. In fact, instead of fending off the imperialistic designs of the United States, the Mounties often found themselves fighting off boredom. The most excitement many constables had on patrol was tracking a locust infestation or spying on the Mormon settlements to see if the stories about polygamy were really true.

Since serious crime was not a problem, the Mounties spent most of their time monitoring the progress of settlement for the Departments of the Interior and Immigration, offering advice to newcomers on soil conditions, and helping to fight prairie fires and outbreaks of disease in both the two- and four-legged populations. In addition, they also dispensed emergency relief to settlers whose crops had failed or were destroyed by fire, though they were careful to confine their generosity to those deemed 'deserving' – people who had proved themselves, by their thrift and industry, to be serious settlers. Echoing sentiments that would be voiced again in the Dirty Thirties, the Department of Immigration warned the Mounties against encouraging immigrants to become dependent on government relief. After all, what Canada wanted was sturdy, independent pioneers – the backbone of a most moral dominion.

Murders were rare on the frontier, but drunken brawling, cattle stealing, prostitution, and liquor selling were rife. Contrary to their Dudley Do-Right image, however, the force adopted a policy of *managing* crime and vice rather than eradicating it. If the Mounties always got their man (or, sometimes, woman), there were numerous occasions when they did not even bother trying. While serious crimes like murder and rape were usually pursued with alacrity, the Mounties tolerated a fairly high level of violence, accepting it as a part of frontier life, and recognizing that, with a small force, they could do little else. In general, as long as crime remained confined to the lower classes and their haunts –

where the Mounties, along with the more respectable elements of society, believed it belonged – the North-West Mounted Police (NWMP) were prepared to look the other way.

The Mounties also tolerated prostitution as long as it remained confined to certain neighbourhoods, where it did not offend the sensibilities of the respectable citizenry, and where they could keep an eye on it. Indeed, in some parts of the West, the men in scarlet did more than keep an eye on the painted ladies, for it was rumoured that the rank and file could be counted on as a brothel's best customers. In 1883, for instance, the *Regina Leader* titillated its readers with reports that the 'red-coat of the Mounted Policeman is seen flashing in and out from these dens at all hours. As no arrests have been made the character of these visits may be easily surmised.'

Whatever the nature of the Mounties' personal relationships with local prostitutes, they believed the 'soiled doves' performed an essential service for the overwhelmingly male population of the West, who might otherwise take liberties with the region's respectable womenfolk. Any attempt to crack down on the prostitutes or their customers was only an invitation to trouble. It made more sense to manage the 'evil' than to try to stamp it out. The NWMP had little time for hypocritical do-gooders like Lethbridge's clergymen, who in 1894 pressed the police to eradicate prostitution altogether. As Superintendent Deane peevishly told his superiors in Ottawa, 'If they would turn their attention to the juvenile depravity and promiscuous fornication that is going on under their own eyes and in their own congregations they would be kept so busy that they would have no time to think of the professional ladies, who at all events are orderly, clean, and on the whole not bad looking.'

By the 1890s moral reformers none the less succeeded in getting the NWMP to be more systematic in their management of vice. Under political pressure, the Mounties began raiding brothels across the West more regularly, offering the prostitutes and their madams a choice of paying fines or leaving town. Given the money to be made at plying their trade, most chose to pay and stay. The result was a situation where prostitution was 'licensed by fine,' an unacceptable compromise to those who wanted the evil expurgated, but a workable and lucrative solution to the prostitutes and the police.

The Mounties' permissive attitude towards prostitution likely stemmed from on-the-job experience, for their efforts to stamp out the liquor trade in the West had illustrated in a very immediate way what could happen when they tried to eradicate vice rather than simply manage it. The liquor trade had brought the Mounties west in the first place, and they persisted in their attempts to control it tightly, rather than to manage it with a few strategic raids every now and then. In 1875 the federal government prohibited the importation, manufacture, and sale of alcohol in the North-west, except, as the act noted, 'for medicinal and sacramental purposes,' or by special permission of the lieutenant-governor of the territory. Those found guilty of violating the law were subject to a fine of up to $300 or six months' imprisonment. These provisions were not instituted with the idea of regulating the Euro-Canadian population, but rather to protect the more numerous aboriginal population in the West from the effects of drink and the depredations of liquor-sellers.

The completion of the Canadian Pacific Railway and the influx of greater numbers of thirsty settlers disrupted the Mounties' enforcement of these regulations. Many newcomers criticized the ban and, not surprisingly, began bootlegging. When they were caught, they complained that prohibition existed only for the poor, since the well-placed and well-to-do received the much-desired lieutenant-governor's permits. Sensitive to charges of favouritism, the territorial government began issuing permits more freely, and the Euro-Canadian population, taking this as a sign of more liberal attitudes, began buying alcohol, not simply for their own consumption (which was what the permits allowed), but for commercial sale.

The West was awash in alcohol as it never had been before. The Mounties' enforcement continued, but they succeeded only in undercutting their own authority. Angry settlers claimed that the NWMP was prosecuting liquor offences as a way of filling their own coffers. Others refused to help the police in any matter at all, and, in 1885, 300 angry Calgarians attached their names to a petition calling for the Mounties to withdraw from their city and all other incorporated towns, 'owing to the arbitrary, capricious and tyrannical manner in which they have administered the law.' Regulating the liquor trade created more problems than it solved, and made the Mounties wary of getting involved in the policing of morals in the future.

They were not so tentative about the morals of the Native peoples, however. The Mounties were instrumental in forcing the Plains Indians onto reserves, though with less vigour than some federal officials expected. Beginning in 1871, the federal government, pressed by many of the Plains Nations, entered into a series of treaty negotiations. A significant number of aboriginals, mostly Plains Cree under Big Bear, Poundmaker, and Piapot, refused to sign treaties and move onto reserves. Instead, in the early 1880s they and their supporters gathered in the Cypress Hills and attempted to maintain their traditional ways. Alarmed by the possibility of a Native revolt, the Department of Indian Affairs (DIA) refused food aid to the growing numbers of starving Indians unless they accepted a treaty. The Mounties, however, gave them minimal rations, reserving full relief for those aboriginals who had already signed treaties and moved onto reserves. As well, they refused to enforce the DIA's pass system, a scheme introduced in 1885 in a bid to restrict Plains Indians' mobility. Instead they preferred to intervene indirectly and selectively by cracking down on horse-stealing. Doing so would not only aid in the 'civilization' of the Indians, but it would also eliminate one of the main reasons for Indians travelling, as well as prevent them from securing more horses – their primary means of conveyance.

Policing on the Urban Frontier

Although police work in cities began several decades before the founding of the Royal North-West Mounted Police, urban policing has failed to attracted the same attention as the colourful traditions of frontier policing. Unlike the Mounties, Canada's urban constables were never celebrated as the undeviating protectors of law and order, 'maintaining the right' against all odds. Instead, they were associated with the mundane tasks of keeping the peace on the unpeaceable streets of nineteenth-century cities. Like the Mounties, however, Canada's urban constables did not convincingly live up to their reputation as 'domestic missionaries' of bourgeois order among the working class. The realities of city policing made it impossible for them to be unswerving agents of control: budgets were tight, personnel was scarce, and recruits were better able to fill their uniforms than meet the expectations of their moral leadership. Anticipating their federal counterparts, municipal police forces concentrated on managing disorderliness, targeting offences such as drunkenness, prostitution, and vagrancy selectively.

Attempting to rid their beats of crime entirely was not only a futile task, but, from the constable's perspective, a counterproductive one, alienating the very people upon whom the police relied for information in investigating more serious crimes. Moreover, as Greg Marquis argues, urban constables were often drawn from the same social ranks as those whom they were expected to police. As working-class men themselves, they were ambivalent about hauling their neighbours into police court for engaging in the same kinds of activities that they themselves indulged in – frequently while on duty. As we will see in Part II, they policed vigorously only to fend off external political pressures.

The response of the working class to the police and the police court in the mid- to late nineteenth century also raises doubts that urban justice can be dismissed as class control. Working people often turned to the police for basic social-services, such as sheltering the homeless and disciplining unruly children. In addition, until the late nineteenth century, when a range of social-service agencies began to emerge in Canada's biggest cities, many poor people took their disputes to the police court, hoping for a resolution. Given the fiscal constraints on policing, the class origins of the police, and the complicated attitude of the working class towards the institutions of urban justice, the urban constable was (in John Weaver's words) a 'reluctant agent of moral order.'

Policing through the Plough and against the Potlatch

The 1885 Northwest Rebellion convinced both the Department of Indian Affairs and the Mounties that the 'gradualist' course they had adopted was unsuited for Canadianizing the Plains. The discontent among the Métis and First Nations in the years before the rebellion had put a damper on western immigration, and, with the bloody events of 1885, the trickle of settlers had dried up completely, endangering the entire project of nation-building. Clearly something had to be done to quell the fears of prospective emigrants, and the best approach was to pursue a more aggressive policy towards the First Nations, ensuring their good behaviour.

To that end, the DIA, under the direction of Hayter Reed, the Indian Commissioner for the Northwest, initiated a policy designed to do nothing less than transform the character and society of the Plains Nations by teaching them to farm. Farming would civilize aboriginals, breaking them of their wandering habits and tying them to the land.

But, just in case they did not immediately see the benefits of sedentary agriculture, Reed retained the DIA's pass system in an attempt to keep aboriginals from leaving reserves. In choosing farming as the means of civilization, Reed reflected a belief in the regenerative capacity of rural life widely shared among moral reformers, especially urban 'child-savers.'

Teaching Indians to farm was not an end in itself. It was part of a larger scheme to undermine the 'tribal system,' and impose Euro-Canadian political and economic values and gender roles. In Reed's eyes, the problem with the tribal system was that it was based on cooperation and collectivism: property and resources were held in common, and everyone worked together to provide the village with a subsistence. There was little incentive for individuals to improve their land or to be particularly industrious, since the fruits of their labour would be distributed equally among all villagers, regardless of how hard each of them worked. So there was little value in teaching Plains Nations to farm if they continued to cultivate their reserve lands in common. The key to civilizing Indians, then, lay in inculcating in them the idea of private property and individual ownership. Reserve lands were therefore subdivided so that Plains Indians would be taught to farm on individual plots of reserve land, each of which would be owned and cultivated by a separate family. Once the burden of tribal cooperation and collectivism was lifted, Reed believed the individual Indian would be free to reap the rewards of his own hard labour. Individual ownership would also break the traditional pattern of redistributing both wealth and foodstuffs. Reed hoped that the better-off would begin to look down on their poorer neighbours who relied on government hand-outs, and eventually would refuse to share the fruits of their own labour with them.

On the West Coast, the attack on aboriginal wealth redistribution and common property took a different tack and was spearheaded by Protestant missionaries, who in 1884 convinced the federal government to criminalize the indigenous ritual known as the 'potlatch.' A communal affair, the potlatch often brought Native peoples from many villages and bands together to celebrate different rites of passage, such as a birth, coming of age, marriage, or death. The gatherings themselves, as well as the practice of gift-giving and feasting that characterized them, served as a public affirmation of the ties of community – among kin, clansfolk, villages, and nations; between those of high and low status; and between generations.

Missionaries branded the potlatch immoral as it was a pagan ceremony which allegedly encouraged profligacy, poverty, and prostitution. Indians spent all their money accumulating goods, only to give them away! Moreover, because of the status attached to sponsoring a potlatch, Native peoples would often go into debt rather than forgo the occasion or hold a more modest ceremony. Worse still, some missionaries claimed that Native men lacking money either stole it or prostituted their wives to get the needed funds. In addition, the ceremony encouraged Native peoples to travel, to live nomadic lives, to neglect their farms, and to take their children out of school – all of which undermined the idealized civilizing effects of the reserve system.

Aboriginal, and particularly Plains, society was also deemed to be problematic because of the gender roles that seemed to operate there. When men were not off hunting buffalo or raiding other villages, they did not seem to do very much that was useful, in Euro-Canadian terms. Indeed, most aboriginal men scorned farming as women's work and were reluctant to take it up. Thus, while transforming Indians into farmers was about imposing certain political values on them, it was also concerned with making aboriginal men conform to Euro-Canadian norms of masculinity. The effort to impose culturally alien gender norms on the Plains Nations through farming was part of a larger project aimed at reproducing the patriarchal nuclear family, which, as we have seen, was carried out with particular clarity and determination in the industrial schools.

Despite their purported 'savagery,' many western Indians none the less embraced agriculture, and by the late 1880s had become so proficient as to pose a real threat to Euro-Canadian agriculturalists. Their achievements should have been viewed as a triumph by the Department of Indian Affairs, proof of the success of their civilizing mission (if not of the Indians' hard work and capacity for change), but this was not the case. In fact, from 1889 to 1897, the department initiated a series of measures designed to *restrict* Native peoples' agricultural productivity. As Sarah Carter demonstrates, the DIA cut down the amount of acreage Plains Indians could have under production and limited the cultivation of commercially valuable cereal crops. Not only would the root crops that were to serve as a replacement allow the Plains Indians to subsist, but the high-maintenance cultivation they required would also teach them diligence and industry.

The concerted effort to turn Plains Indians into peasant farmers after they had demonstrated their ability to compete with their white neighbours points to Euro-Canadians' general ambivalence about the civilizing mission. Though the mandate of the DIA was to Canadianize aboriginals, socializing them to capitalist and patriarchal family values, it was clear that many Euro-Canadians were uncomfortable with the prospect of Indians actually becoming part of the larger Canadian family. Whether proficient farmers, who had learned their lessons a little too well, or 'uncivilized' people, who refused to submit to religious or secular authorities, they could still appear as threats to Euro-Canadians.

For all the talk about Canadianizing the Indians and improving their condition, the moral regulation of aboriginals was ultimately not about changing the racial order of things. Instead, it reproduced the existing pecking order, with Indians at the bottom and Euro-Canadians on top.

Even the industrial schools, institutions expressly charged with assimilating aboriginal children, did this. Like the plains farmers, graduates of the industrial schools often succeeded beyond expectations, thereby eliciting complaints from Euro-Canadians who feared competition in a tight labour market. As a result, after 1896 both the schools and the Department of Indian Affairs shifted the goals of their educational policy away from academic subjects. Instead, as Jean Barman reveals, Indian girls were taught how to make baskets and to do laundry by 'boiling their clothes in coal-oil tins to which wooden handles have been attached.' By the first decades of the twentieth century, instead of assimilating First Nations children so that they could be integrated into Euro-Canadian society, Indian education was designed to allow them to eke out a marginal existence on the reserves.

Not all of these regulatory measures were successful in the late nineteenth century. The permit and pass systems were virtually unenforceable, as was the law against the potlatch on the West Coast. Hobbled by a lack of personnel on the ground, and in many cases a lack of will to enforce an unpopular measure, the Department of Indian Affairs's efforts to get rid of these 'worse than useless custom[s]' were frequently met by open resistance on the part of Native people. While some taunted the government, virtually daring it to charge them, more commonly aboriginals responded to race-specific regulations with wily subversion and strategic accommodation. As a result, few Indians were charged with potlatching before 1896. Ultimately, the federal government and the missionaries worried that having a statute on the books that was not enforced raised general doubts about the law in people's minds, and undermined its authority and that of the people, such as Indian agents and missionaries, who were charged with upholding it.

Even the industrial schools were not the totalizing institutions their designers had hoped they would be. Despite an 1894 law compelling Indian children to attend school, most who had access to one refused to go. Industrial schools never reached much more than a third of eligible Native children. Moreover, those who did attend often did not complete the entire program of study. Even while enrolled, students often left to visit their parents, and vice versa, and changes were sometimes made to the curriculum in response to parental complaints. In addition, English was not as hegemonic as the Department of Indian Affairs would have liked. Many students continued to speak in their own tongues, often *encouraged* by clergy who were anxious to hone their own skills in indigenous languages, and who had gone to the trouble of writing Native catechisms.

Tracing attempts to incorporate aboriginals of the West into the new dominion provides only the most visible example of how the task of building a nation was inseparable from building the character of its inhabitants. Something as simple as teaching First Nations peoples to farm served a disciplinary function, laden as the lessons were with Euro-Canadian ideas about private property, gender roles, and the family. However, it also illustrates our general argument that the effects of moral regulation rarely conform to its stated purposes.

Disciplining Canada's 'Waifs and Strays'

Like aboriginals, non-Native children were subjected to a regulatory regime aimed at civilizing their untamed passions through a system of publicly funded schools. And as was the case with Native children, legislation had little effect in shaping school attendance. Instead, the rhythms of work and the family economy largely determined when children went to school, and how much schooling they received when they did show up. In the countryside, attendance patterns were shaped by the seasonal cycle: boys, valuable during seeding and harvesting, could usually be spared from their round of chores in the winter. Farm girls, on the other hand, attended less in the winter, staying home to care for younger siblings who could not travel to school in the harsh weather. The pattern of attendance for urban youngsters was irregular as well, but not for the same reasons. Instead, it was shaped by the availability of wage work for the children themselves and for other family members. In general, in both the city and the country, children of more prosperous families were more likely to attend, and to attend more frequently. Thus, class, as well as region, influenced attendance patterns far more profoundly than did the law – particularly since truant officers were almost non-existent, except in large cities such as Toronto, where, significantly, they were made part of the police *morality* squad in 1893. Even there, officers were up against the transience of working-class people, a fact that made it difficult to even tell whether a child was truant or had simply moved away. They were further stymied by traditional working-class suspicion of authority. Thus neighbours in the know preferred to pretend not to be.

The gap between attendance law and its enforcement was no secret, since the Department of Education trumpeted it every year in its annual report. Nor was the whereabouts of these missing children a great mystery: they were working as domestics, farm labourers, miners, news-sellers, hawkers, and pedlars. Despite this, Canada's child-savers focused their attention on a relatively small minority of child workers – those who toiled in its larger factories. Most were over twelve (the maximum age to which compulsory schooling applied in the late nineteenth century), and worked in the textile, clothing, woodworking, food-processing, and tobacco industries. To manufacturers, children were desirable employees: the combination of nimble fingers, small bodies, and low wages made them perfect for repetitious work in profit-driven factories crowded with tricky machinery. But the same cost-cutting measures that led manufacturers to hire children instead of adults also meant that the conditions the workers faced left much to be desired. As the testimony at the 1887–8 Royal Commission on the Relations

of Labour and Capital revealed, nineteenth-century factories could be squalid, dark, airless, and, above all, dangerous places, where workers breathed in dust, cringed at the
endless clatter of gears and looms, and were maimed or
killed by machinery.

The horrors of Canada's 'dark satanic mills' moved legislators in Ontario and Quebec into action. In the mid-1880s,
both provinces restricted child labour to boys over twelve
and girls over fourteen, and limited the hours they could
work to ten per day, or sixty per week (except in cases of
'breakdown' or exigency). The law applied only to establishments employing more than twenty people. Securing
compliance to the factories acts was difficult. Both provinces appointed too few factory inspectors for the task, and
those who did make the rounds were frustrated by uncoop-
erative employers and employees who lied about the ages
and working hours of their youngest operatives. Factory
owners wanted cheap labour, and working-class parents
needed the extra income or welcomed the discipline factory work imposed on otherwise idle and unruly children.
According to Lorna Hurl, as long as children were disciplined, the institutional context (school or factory) did not
really matter to most parents. In the end, as Chad Gaffield
demonstrates for the lumber-mill town of Hawkesbury,
the elimination of child labour by the late nineteenth century was as much the result of structural changes in the
economy, as of changing attitudes towards schooling and of
compulsory-education laws.

While public schooling did not achieve all that its supporters had claimed it would, the education provided by
the province's industrial schools actually attained unstated
objectives by reinforcing class divisions. As Paul Bennett's
evidence suggests, an industrial-school education seemed
aimed at guaranteeing that working-class children would
become working-class adults. The boys were trained not to
be 'bookkeepers and clerks,' as they would have been in the
public system, but manual labourers. Thus, industrial edu-

cation reproduced class relations among the 'waifs and strays' of central Canadian cities, just as it reinforced racial and economic dominance among aboriginals.

The ethic of care that was supposed to animate institutions for children and women proved similarly hollow. Neglected and delinquent children and wayward women were supposed to be reformed through remedial training in a setting modelled on the family, where they could learn to know their place, obey their elders and betters, and contribute to the family economy. In the end, however, the family model and maternalism were hobbled by overcrowding and a lack of funds and sensitivity among the institutions' staff. More fundamentally, however, institutions such as the Victoria Industrial School and the Mercer Reformatory failed because of the impossibility of making what were coercive environments into 'homes.' The 'velvet glove' of the family model might have hidden the coercive aspects of these institutions from the public, as Carolyn Strange has suggested, but it could not cushion the inmates from the iron fist of the state.

The failure of industrial schooling for non-Native children gave impetus to child-savers like Toronto's J.J. Kelso, who opposed institutional care. If neglected and delinquent children needed remedial family training, Kelso argued, then why not place them with real families, rather than in institutions that were modelled on the family? He also proposed that that responsibility be given to the new voluntary society he founded in 1891: the Children's Aid Society of Toronto. The provincial government, moved as much by cost-cutting considerations as Kelso's strong case, agreed, and in 1893 passed legislation that changed the direction of child welfare in the province and, over the following decades, the country. The Act for the Prevention of Cruelty to, and better Protection of Children partially shifted responsibility for making children good from the hands of the state over to private, voluntary societies that would be governed by the Superintendent of Neglected and Dependent Children – the first of whom was J.J. Kelso. Children's Aid Societies (CAS) were established across Ontario, and eventually across Canada, as industrial schools and state involvement in the moral regulation of children declined. When the state did reassert itself in with the passage of the first Juvenile Delinquents Act in 1908, it made the CAS an active partner in the new juvenile-court system. As we will see, the cooperation between public and private institutions and legal and non-legal personnel marked the beginnings of what Dorothy Chunn calls 'socialized justice,' a concept that was also extended to women in 1913 with the establishment of the first women's courts.

Good Girls Don't

Innovative legislation designed to protect girls and women also fell short of expectations. On the surface, it seemed to embody progressive attitudes towards women and their right to be free from sexual interference. In practice, the enforcement of these laws was selective, filtered through prevailing attitudes about race, ethnicity, class, and gender. Legislation that was meant to protect women actually worked to police their behaviour, reinforcing the idea that women fell into two categories: the innocent victim and the designing vixen.

In seduction cases, women found that their behaviour was policed and scrutinized as much as that of their alleged male seducers. As Karen Dubinsky argues, parents used the law to force reluctant suitors to 'do the right thing' and marry a pregnant daughter; however, they also found the law useful in breaking up relationships they deemed unsuitable. There was nothing like the threat of criminal prosecution to throw cold water on even the most passionate relationship. Love might conquer all, but parents, with the wieght of the state behind them, packed heavier artillery. Rather than protect women, criminalizing seduction provided parents, and particularly fathers, with yet another means to police their daughters' behaviour.

Seduction trials publicly communicated the standards of female character. Cases turned on whether women were of 'previously chaste character.' Here was a double standard: while female chastity could determine the disposition of a seduction case, male chastity – something that might have been equally relevant – was not at issue. Women were asked about previous relationships with men, their church attendance and employment, and, in some cases, their parents' moral conduct. They were also queried intensively about how the seduction had occurred. Although consent was not supposed to be an issue in these cases, women tried to convince juries they had had to be 'coaxed' into sex, while male defendants tried to prove that the woman in question was more than willing. Dredging up one or more of her ex-lovers usually proved the point.

The close scrutiny afforded to women's sexual pasts in conjunction with the higher standard of proof required in criminal trials resulted in a dismal conviction rate. Civil cases for seduction were successful 90 per cent of the time, but, between 1900 and 1910, only 9 per cent of criminal prosecutions succeeded. Women were ten times *less* likely to win if they went through the criminal, as opposed to the civil, courts.

Not surprisingly, the double standard of sexual behaviour continued to govern the enforcement of Canada's rape laws. Even more than civil trials for seduction, rape trials focused on the matter of the alleged victim's sexual character. Again, defendants tried to undermine their accusers' credibility by raising questions about past sexual conduct. Had they consorted with other men? how many? and to what end? Had they resisted the accused's advances? how much? Other more subtle factors were also at play. Class, race, and ethnicity defined respectability in the courtroom as much as they did outside it, and defence counsel deployed every stereotype they could muster to strengthen their case. For instance, because domestic servant Emma Foam had accepted a stranger's invitation to dinner, she was deemed 'fallen,' and her story of rape was not believed by the jury. However, Carolyn Strange shows that race, ethnicity, and class shaped *men's* credibility as much as it did women's 'rapability.' Working-class southern and eastern Europeans as well as black men were considered to have 'animalistic' passions, while Chinese men, though effeminate, were believed to find white women endlessly fascinating. The enforcement of the law against rape was selective, reinforcing both gender norms and the dominant norms about race, ethnicity, and class.

Women also continued to comprise an overwhelming majority of those arrested and convicted of prostitution and prostitution-related offences. Those most vulnerable to prosecution and conviction were single, poor, and illiterate, frequently listing domestic service as their occupation. In Toronto, Irish Catholic women were overrepresented among those taken in, making up almost 70 per cent of those arrested for prostitution in 1865. In Halifax, black women comprised 40 per cent of those arrested for prostitution between 1864 and 1873, at a time when the blacks made up just 3 per cent of the Nova Scotia population. As was the case with the enforcement of the laws against rape, the profile of arrests for prostitution and prostitution-related offences confirms that legal moral regulation both reflected and reinforced existing social norms about gender, race, ethnicity, and class.

Conclusion

In this chapter we have mapped out the gulf that separated the law in action from the law on the books. The Mounties exemplified the high-minded idealism of legal moral regulation, but they also show how campaigns to regulate morality through the law failed by their own standards. No matter how smart their uniforms or proud their bearing, the reality was that the Mounties were still a force of several hundred men, charged with policing a vast expanse of territory populated by a more numerous aboriginal population and a growing number of European settlers. Not surprisingly, they, as well as their municipal counterparts, adopted a pragmatic (and much less heroic or glamorous) approach to controlling vice and crime and to colonizing 'savages' – whether they were on the reserves or in the inner cities.

Like the Mounties, government administrators charged with civilizing the aboriginal population had set equally lofty goals for themselves: the complete transformation of an entire population of Native Indians into Canadian citizens. Nothing less, they believed, would save a 'vanishing race.' Their noble ends did not, however, preclude them from using some ignoble means. Still, the DIA's coercive tactics did not guarantee its regulatory agenda would be kept. Confronted with Native farmers who became remarkably successful, the DIA, in response to public pressure from whites, took steps to block aboriginal peoples' progress. In the end, a policy, indeed an entire bureaucracy, dedicated to assimilating Native peoples did exactly the opposite.

Regulatory schemes imposed on Canada's aboriginal population were soon translated for its non-Natives, particularly children, women, and the very poor. Though compulsory education and the Factories Act, as well as the curriculum in place at the industrial schools, were all designed to improve the condition of working-class children, they ultimately reinforced class boundaries, just as the DIA's efforts at moral regulation solidified the existing racial hierarchy. Similarly, the legislation aimed at protecting women ended up stigmatizing them, reproducing gender norms as well as racial, ethnic, and class stereotypes.

PART II: ENVISIONING MORALITY, 1896–1919

3

Recruiting the State

In the 1890s, one of the more curious controversies in Canadian history – the debate over the morality of Sunday streetcar service – mushroomed from a spat in Toronto civic politics into a successful parliamentary campaign to reinforce sabbath observance across the country. The achievements and frustrations of the sabbatarians, as these reformers were called, symbolized the most notable characteristics of legal moral regulation in Canada at the turn of the century. Presbyterian and Methodist ministers, as well as concerned lay people, led campaigns to uplift morality with the help of the state. More important, the national government began to listen to demands that the state take a more active position in regulating the moral life of the nation. As rates of non-Protestant and (in the case of Jews, and small numbers of Chinese) non-Christian immigration rose, demands that the 'traditional' sabbath be legally regulated even converted some Christian Canadians who were otherwise dubious about state interference in individual pleasures.

Lobbyists' successful introduction of new restrictions against the consumption of alcohol and various forms of commercialized vice (including prostitution, gambling, and drugs) did not translate into uniform or effective enforcement, however. For one thing, individuals who felt that they had a right to determine their own pleasures violated new morals laws flagrantly and clandestinely; for another, law-enforcement agencies were not only insufficiently funded to flush out immorality, but ambivalent about the wisdom of outright repression. At the provincial level, the Quebec government flatly refused to impose morality laws set by the secular federal government. Roman Catholic leaders' discomfort with Protestant moralists, coupled with the church's historic jurisdiction over moral matters, meant that priests and bishops were no more enthusiastic than Quebec politicians to embrace Protestant-dominated moral-reform lobbying. Concerned about the moral well-being of their parishioners, they preferred to work within French Catholic channels of moral suasion. While new and more stringent laws were introduced to police the nation's morals at the turn of the century, Canadians of different faiths, and in different regions, continued to disagree about the best means of making citizens good.

By the late nineteenth century, long-standing moral causes, such as temperance and sexual purity, were given new spins as politically astute moral-reform organizations called not only on individuals to improve, but on the state to throw its resources behind the cause of social improvement. This coalition of largely Protestant reform groups (which historians have described as the 'social purity movement') presented a vision of moral uplift for the entire country. Leaders set out to transform the state from an impassive laissez-faire institution to an interventionist moral watchdog. Challenging existing laws, devising new ones, and embarrassing law enforcers into stricter morals policing were their favoured tactics. Although lobbyists identified a host of moral problems requiring regulation, we will focus on a handful to illustrate how social purity advocates managed to align state powers of legal regulation to their reform agenda by the early twentieth century.

The 'Melancholy Nature of the Canadian Sunday'

In a period when the hunger for profits pushed big business to extract more and more labour from their employees, craft unions' successes in negotiating a nine-hour workday and Sundays off were not inconsiderable. Labouring people jealously guarded Sunday as their one free day of the week, and they were backed by the Christian calendar, which designated it as a divinely sanctioned day of rest. Since workers, not employers, determined how they would spend their precious free time, the prospect of unregulated Sundays raised troubling questions in the minds of those who worried that Christianity was losing its hold over Canadians, particularly urbanites. In cities, a growing number of tempting alternatives to religious observance, including saloons, vaudeville houses, amusement parks, and pleasure-boat excursions, beckoned workers with time on their hands away from home and church. The tempest over the Toronto Street Railroad Company's application for a Sunday licence grew out of these concerns. After several plebiscites, a stream of letters to city newspapers, and a protracted four-year political battle, the streetcar company won. On 23 May 1897, 45,000 Torontonians boarded the city's first Sunday streetcars.

Historian Sharon Meen suggests that this tiff might have blown over had the Citizens' Central Anti–Sunday Car Committee folded its tents and admitted defeat. Instead, a new lobby group, the Ontario Lord's Day Alliance (OLDA), took up the standard and expanded the committee's work province-wide. After initially courting working-class support for their efforts (someone, after all, had to drive those trams and run those vaudeville houses), the OLDA was unsympathetic to testy claims that workers had a right to do as they pleased on Sundays. More reasoned arguments from those who advocated the moral benefits of 'rational' recreation fell flat too. To the OLDA's chagrin, existing forms of regulation failed to curb the commercialization of the sabbath. Even in Toronto, where the country's first morality squad (in the person of Inspector David Archibald) was established in 1887, police officers were more concerned with drunks and wife-beaters than they were with Sunday vendors. Faced with sluggish enforcement and blatant infringement of existing regulations at the provincial level, the OLDA decided to go national by the turn of the twentieth century.

The campaign for a federal law to standardize the right and wrong ways Canadians could spend their time on Sundays was short and sweet. From 1903 to 1906, branches across the country focused their lobbying efforts on one target – Laurier's Liberal government. In letters and petitions, stricter sabbath-observance legislation was proposed as a means to preserve British traditions, both from American-style commercialism and from Europeans' notorious taste for pleasures of the flesh. Without stricter laws, the Dominion Lord's Day Alliance predicted that the Canadian sabbath would degenerate into 'a day of turmoil and abominations, open shows and open theatres.' Without solid support from French-Canadian members of Parliament (many of whom complained about federal interference in the simple pleasures of life), Minister of Justice Allen Aylesworth none the less introduced the nationwide Lord's Day Act in 1906.

In short order, the sweetness of victory soured somewhat. Before the ink was dry on the new act, the government of Quebec passed legislation to declare that the Lord's Day Act would not interfere with 'all such liberties as are recognized by the custom of this province.' Elsewhere in the country, notably in western towns, where the male population far exceeded that of women, and where eastern and southern European cultural traditions fostered more relaxed attitudes towards Sunday enjoyments, local support for the federal act was little more than perfunctory. Cities such as Montreal and Calgary continued to enjoy dubious reputations as 'wide-open' towns where the turn of a calendar page was hardly considered reason enough to stop having fun. Only in the country's Protestant strongholds, particularly in Ontario and the Maritimes, did the act receive moral support from local authorities. So successful were the sabbatarians in Toronto, where the Sunday spat began, that a traveller pronounced it 'one of the most unpleasantly righteous cities I was ever caught in on a Sunday.'

'The' Social Evil

Social purity reformers were not content to leave the other six days of the week unregulated. At any time, 'mere pleasure seekers' might find their base desires satisfied by those who offered a dizzying array of immoral diversions, the chief among them being commercial sex and alcohol. The brothel and the saloon had long been targets of moral disgust, but both had been considered more-or-less-inevitable features of city and town life through most of the nineteenth century. Efforts to suppress prostitution had been limited to token raids on obnoxious brothels, and to police crack-downs on rowdy taverns. Federal legislation did empower localities to vote themselves 'dry,' and municipalities imposed restrictions on grog shops, but prostitution seemed to defy regulation. Protestant lobbyists rose to the challenge. As Mariana Valverde and others have argued, Canadians, like their British and U.S. counterparts, inflated prostitution into the master problem of the age – 'the social evil.' Thus, prostitution presented a special challenge to ambitious reformers.

The highest hurdles they faced were doubts that state intervention would ever eliminate prostitution. First, there were the actual participants in the sex trade. In every Canadian city, pockets of urban space, usually near railway terminals, wharves, taverns, and rooming-house districts, were known by locals and travellers alike as places where men could buy sex. On the Prairies, Euro-Canadian men visited Native women, hoping for sexual services which respectable white women, still rare in remote and northern settlements, would not provide. Prostitution was highly visible, especially in working-class districts, where street-walking was the

cheapest form of advertisement. In mining towns and logging camps, bosses were inclined to turn a blind eye to
camp-followers unless they inspired fights between the
men. Whenever the sex trade erupted into drunken disorderliness or violence, police agents were likely to swoop
down, but, so long as neighbours did not complain, prostitution was still grudgingly tolerated in most late-nineteenth-century cities and towns.

The very people charged with enforcing laws – local
police officers in towns and cities, and the Royal Northwest
Mounted Police in the largely unsettled West – remained
unconvinced that well-intentioned legal reforms would
make a dent in the trade. Admitting that this was standard
police practice was another matter, however. Some policemen who tolerated prostitution were undoubtedly corrupt,
as social purity advocates habitually charged. Red-light districts were operated by madams who skimmed their profits
into the pockets of policemen prepared to look the other
way or to warn them of raids. Ironically, prostitutes con-
tributed to the regulation of vice and crime by feeding
police officers information about suspicious customers and
other shady characters associated with the sex trade. Law-
enforcement officials' cynicism grew out of their street
smarts: prostitution could be suppressed through the law,
or squeezed into certain parts of cities, but the police could
never wipe out commercialized sex.

Undaunted by the prospect of unwilling enforcers (and
an ever-eager clientele), a wide range of social purity advocates worked tirelessly to convince Canadians that something could and *ought* to be done to rid the country of
commercialized sexual vice. Social purity advocates successfully constructed prostitution as a symbol of all that was
wrong about modern, increasingly urbanized, Canada. By
the late 1890s, they claimed that 'white slavery,' a troubling
new version of prostitution, had made its way to Canada. As
they alleged, unscrupulous women and men (typically,
though not always 'foreigners') inveigled innocent young

white women into sexual slavery. Through their melodramatic stories of last-minute rescues and tragic seductions, social purity lobbyists encouraged Canadians to drop the conventional image of the hard-bitten, drink-sodden prostitute in favour of the virginal girl, forced to service men of all classes and races against her will. Viewing themselves as good Christian soldiers, well-meaning women and men marched into battle in the 'war against white slavery,' as one famous tract described their mission. The terrain they sought for their battles was not just that of public opinion, but that of the law.

Their first step was to educate the public, and politicians in particular. The 1892 Criminal Code had established penalties for a range of sexual offences against women and girls, but members of the Protestant clergy, and women in the YWCA, the National Council of Women of Canada (NCWC), and the WCTU were convinced that Canadian girls were still not sufficiently protected against a growing international sexual slave trade. The most effective organization to bring news of the trade to Canadian audiences was the Temperance, Prohibition, and Moral Reform Department of the Methodist Church of Canada, formed in 1902 and headed by the Reverend S.D. Chown. Five years later, the Methodists found allies in the Presbyterians, who set up the Board of Moral and Social Reform. By 1908, it was joined by the Moral and Social Reform Council of Canada, a largely Ontario-based organization headed by Presbyterian Dr John Shearer and Methodist Reverend T. Albert Moore, both leading members of the sabbatarian movement. As part of its broader mandate to uplift the moral tone of Canadian society, the council spawned in 1912 the National Committee for the Suppression of the White Slave Traffic.

Avowedly Protestant and anglophilic in outlook, these organizations earned few French-Canadian adherents outside of Montreal's pockets of Protestantism. The Roman Catholic clergy was equally concerned about prostitution, but more suspicious of the state's capacity or fitness to govern this delicate area of sexual impropriety. Historians have been unable to verify white-slavery allegations through police or court records. Nevertheless, social purity advocates were sufficiently troubled by the melodramatic anecdotes breathlessly related in international conferences to launch an all-out campaign against the trade in Canada.

Two events in 1911 touched off a moral panic which added impetus to demands to legislate against the social evil. *The War on the White Slave Trade*, a collection of sensational articles published that year, included one by Reverend Shearer, who claimed that Canada's 'traffic in girls,' conducted largely by 'foreign' men, catered to both a Canadian and an international market. Many readers were roused to action. In less than a year after the book's publication, the NCWC White Slavery committee president eagerly noted that public support had swelled considerably. An investigation of prostitution in Winnipeg in 1911 was no less disturbing. Evidence presented to the provincially appointed Roblin Commission confirmed that vice thrived in this booming city. In 1909, the Winnipeg mayor had approved a plan, cooked up by the police chief and the city's madams, to establish an official red-light zone, far away from the more salubrious sections of the city. As historian James Gray notes, the solution was soon declared a flop. The working-class residents of Point Douglas, the area designated for commercial sex, complained that their neighbourhood had turned into a modern Sodom and Gomorrah. In response, the police merely tightened the screws of regulation. The brothels could remain, but red lights had to be extinguished, house numbers had to be smaller, and the practice of accosting locals and their children had to be stopped. Every two weeks, prostitutes were required to pass a medical inspection, and if they were found to be carrying venereal disease they were put out of business until cured.

This peculiar form of legal moral regulation, in which

agents of the law regulated *illegal* activities, was popular with prostitutes and their clients, but neighbours and religious authorities were appalled at the goings-on. The area became so notorious that it quickly became a tourist site, where the curious could gawk at scantily clad and saucy-mouthed prostitutes, while the game could purchase sexual services. Trouble brewed whenever customers, often drunk and boisterous, failed to respect the official boundaries of the red-light district. By the summer of 1910, neighbouring communities, local churches and city missions, and, finally, national moral-reform organizations decided to fight back. Social purity reformers turned Winnipeg into a test case: would Canadians tolerate loosely regulated prostitution, or would they take a stand against officially sanctioned immorality? In Reverend Shearer's opinion, published in the Toronto *Globe*, Winnipeg's legal toleration of prostitution had produced a 'moral cesspool, the stench of which is making itself felt to the discredit of Winnipeg throughout the Dominion and elsewhere.' Feeling the heat from all corners, civic politicians requested that the province investigate accusations of corruption and white slavery.

News accounts of the hearings held by the commission provided Winnipeggers and Canadians elsewhere with titillating breakfast reading. Evidence was aired by police officers, residents, concerned citizens, and prostitutes themselves (no self-declared customers testified). The police readily admitted that they used their regulatory powers to moderate, rather than to suppress, the sex trade. In its January 1911 report, the inquiry confirmed that the Winnipeg police had indeed instituted a 'policy of toleration of the offence in a limited area, with regulations as to conduct.' But problems occurred after regulatory lapses had led to 'the disturbance of peace and good order in the locality, a menace to morals and great depreciation in value of property of the neighbouring residents.' In a surprising move, Mayor Robson, ignoring the commission's condemnation of his policy, boldly ran for re-election – and won!

Evidently Winnipeggers (at least those men and women who voted) were troubled more by the laxity and incompetence of police regulation than by the segregation and toleration of prostitution *per se*. The investigation of Winnipeg's commercial sex industry failed to confirm claims that the city operated a white slavery trade, but it did add momentum to the movement for harsher federal legislation against prostitution.

Legislating against the Social Evil

Politicians could not fail to notice the furore. In 1912, Robert Borden's new Conservative government was flooded with briefs, reports, and letters, all calling on the state to crack down on white slavers. Justice Minister Charles Doherty met Reverend Moore to assure him that the federal government would treat the matter seriously. In short order, the government announced a series of amendments to the Criminal Code to combat white slavery, including stiffer penalties for existing offences and new categories of moral infractions. As is often the case with morals legislation, the onus of proof fell on the accused, not on the Crown: suspected offenders were presumed to be guilty unless they could prove otherwise. John McLaren's research shows that keeping or 'being found in' a 'common bawdy house' (brothel) had been an offence under the 1892 Code, but the 1913 amendment now empowered police to presume that landlords or mistresses were brothel-keepers simply by virtue of their owning or running an establishment where sex between women and men occurred for a fee. Keepers of rooming-houses or hotels could be arrested if they failed to evict tenants who used their premises for 'immoral purposes.' Although 'procuring a female for the purposes of prostitution' was already on the books, second offenders now faced the possibility of being whipped in addition to serving jail time. Police officers required no warrant to arrest suspected procurers, and charges could be laid no matter what the age of alleged victims.

The aim of these new measures was to shift responsibility for prostitution from the women themselves, as the common law had traditionally done, to those who exploited and profited from prostitutes' labour. Social-purity reformers could congratulate themselves for having translated the white-slavery panic into legislative action, since a section of the revised code made it an offence to conceal a female in a brothel, or to entice new immigrants into becoming prostitutes. If white slavery stories required imagination to supply the details, so did the vaguely worded legislative amendments which introduced the offence of exercising 'control, direction, or influence' over females for the purposes of prostitution. More concrete were the anti-pimping provisions. The 1913 amendment made 'living wholly or in part on the avails of prostitution' an offence for anyone without visible means of support who lived or habitually associated with prostitutes.

The Criminal Code amendments of 1913, along with several further amendments passed in 1915, represent one of the most successful legal-reform lobbying efforts in Canadian history. Their remarkable influence over public policy illustrates that the national government was more willing than it had been in the nineteenth century to legalize religious lobbyists' moral agendas. In the early part of the twentieth century, evangelical leaders such as Reverend Shearer of the Moral and Social Reform Council of Canada could literally march into cabinet ministers' offices and tell them how they ought to legislate.

The Demon Rum

Prostitution was rarely discussed at the turn of the century without concerns about alcohol being voiced in the same breath. Brothels and taverns were cheek-by-jowl in inner cities, but no matter how remote a bawdy-house, purveyors, prostitutes, and customers all took booze for granted as a feature of the business. Indeed, James Gray argues that, in many parts of the country where prostitution was more or less tolerated, drinking trumped prostitution as a social problem, crying out for a regulatory solution. This was particularly the case in the West and in urban wards where single, itinerant men, many of them young 'foreigners,' worked hard and played hard. Prohibitionists attracted adherents by appealing to widespread concerns about working-class men's most visible form of recreation – public drinking. Thus the movement to enforce prohibition provides another example of a regulatory campaign which attacked one thing (alcohol) by targeting specific forms of behaviour, particular types of people, and certain public spaces.

Alcohol was damnable because of its association with illicit sex and masculine rowdiness, but its consumption was also condemned as a sign of moral weakness connected to a host of other sins, including gambling, profanity, smoking, and idleness. For strict prohibitionists, alcohol was an evil that weakened the moral fibre of even the toughest, most upright souls. For more moderate temperance advocates, certain types of people, already assumed to be weak-willed, had to be kept from drink, for their own and others' good. This was the pretext under which Indians had been 'protected' from enjoying the same drinking rights which other Canadians exercised. Non-Native Canadians would not experience such restrictions until the early twentieth century (and then, only briefly).

From the vantage point of the late twentieth century, the drinking patterns of Canadians from a century ago are astonishing. Cities and towns, from the Maritimes to British Columbia, let alone the Klondike, were chock-a-block with taverns, saloons, and cheap hotels where the largely male and working-class clientele sought solace in bottles and conviviality among fellow male drinkers and 'fast' women. The 1896 Royal Commission on the Liquor Traffic determined that the average Canadian consumed just under one-half gallon of alcohol per day. British Columbians drank a gallon each! Licensing regulations introduced in the late nineteenth century had reduced some of the worst drinking dives in settled parts of the country, but ports, mining towns, logging areas, and railway centres – in short, places where rootless working men gathered in large numbers – were notorious for their unrestricted, disorderly drinking practices. In turn-of-the-century cities, unsanitary drinking water still provided a good excuse to consume alcohol, but working men felt they needed no excuse, save thirst, exhaustion, and boredom.

Women and otherwise respectable Canadians were, however, partial to a drop too. Prostitutes were usually the only women who dared to drink in saloons and hotels, and any woman who drank publicly knew that she risked gaining an unsavoury reputation. Yet poor women gulped pots of beer in their cramped quarters, while respectable ladies sipped sherry and wine in their dining-rooms. Gentlemen could quaff port and whisky with their cigars in their clubs or at the bars of fine hotels without fear of running into working men, poor immigrants, or Indians. In recognizing these spatially and demographically mixed cultures of imbibing, the temperance movement did not so much call for an end to drinking as it aimed to regulate the habits of low-life people in low-life places.

The Woman's Christian Temperance Union (WCTU), a leading force in the campaign against prostitution since the organization's founding in Canada in 1874, was the foremost group dedicated to combating alcohol and its related social and medical problems. Despite its long-standing efforts to instigate a legislative solution to the problem of drunkenness, the WCTV achieved little more than moral victories in the nineteenth century. The Scott Act of 1878 had allowed localities to hold prohibition plebiscites, but it lacked enforcement provisions. As a result, only the Maritimes and rural pockets of Ontario, and Prince Edward

Island, in particular, exercised the option. But regulation through local option had made a mockery of the act. Boozing in cities like Halifax, the only place in Nova Scotia where one could buy a drink legally, became even more disorderly as customers from dry areas travelled to wet towns to slake their thirst. By the 1890s, the WCTU and their brethren in the Dominion Alliance for the Total Suppression of the Liquor Traffic faced another blow when the 1896 royal commission recommended against instituting federal prohibition. The two organizations took a deep breath and tried again – this time pleading their case to Laurier's Liberal government.

The Liberals made their triumphant way to the government benches partly through the support of prohibitionists from Ontario, Manitoba, and the Maritimes. Laurier had been a long-time opponent of prohibition (as were the majority of Quebeckers, whose attitudes towards alcohol more closely resembled Europeans'), but he agreed to hold a national plebiscite on the issue in 1898. Historian Sharon Cook notes that the Alliance and the WCTU had regarded the plebiscite as morally, if not legally, binding, but the government clearly felt differently. Canadians were asked: 'Are you in favour of passing an Act prohibiting the importation, manufacture, or sale of spirits, wine, ale, cider, and all other alcoholic liquors for use as a beverage?' An overwhelming majority of Ontarians and Maritimers voted in favour of prohibition, but British Columbians were evenly divided, and voters in Quebec turned it down by a margin of five to one. Since only 44 per cent of eligible voters had voiced their opinions, Laurier decided to bury the issue. Robbed of a federal victory, temperance forces regrouped at the provincial level, where they began to make greater headway in their lobbying efforts.

The WCTU and the Dominion Alliance continued to prime the public to adopt the temperance cause. They gave speeches, wrote tracts, and recruited supporters, from babes in arms to reformed alcoholics, in order to further their mission. Women of the WCTU never proselytized without clutching a pack of 'pledge cards.' These were informal contracts, signed by converts, who promised to regulate themselves: 'I hereby promise, with the help of God, to abstain from the use of all intoxicating liquors ...' Some cards included clauses regarding tobacco and profanity.

The WCTU turned temperance into a gender issue by stressing the harm caused by drunken men who left their wives and children destitute or, worse still, brutalized their dependants. One of their typical claims was that alcohol 'turns men into demons and makes women easy prey to lust.' WCTU women campaigned that a vote for prohibition was a vote against violence, poverty, and crime. Sweeping claims such as these persuaded many men to offer public support for the WCTU. Others who resented any form of interference with masculine liberties preferred to translate 'WCTU' as 'Women who Constantly Torment Us.' As campaigns to introduce women's suffrage gained strength, hostile anti-suffragists realized that votes for women might well translate into votes against the bar, and against masculine liberties in general. Their suspicions would prove to be correct.

The first provincial victory came in 1902, not surprisingly in Prince Edward Island, where the Scott Act had been implemented most effectively. Elsewhere, local chapters of the WCTU and the Dominion Alliance worked to increase the number of jurisdictions exercising the local dry option, and to make it easier for citizens to vote their localities alcohol-free. Through such efforts, Nova Scotia went completely dry. In the meantime, membership in temperance organizations grew, making it harder for politicians to ignore calls for liquor restrictions. In Ontario alone, there were 9,000 WCTU members by 1914. In every province but Quebec, where bishops and priests led their own local campaigns against drunkenness, temperance had become a political force to be reckoned with.

The First World War turned out to be an important catalyst for the introduction of temperance acts at the provincial and federal levels. The wartime sense of a national emergency gave a critical boost to prohibition advocates. After all, the Dominion Alliance argued, drunken men made poor soldiers, and money spent on boozing could be spent more wisely on the war effort. Not only would prohibition solve a host of social problems, as proponents had claimed for years, but now it would help win the war too.

Beginning in 1916, every government in the nation slapped unprecedented restrictions on the sale, trade, and consumption of alcohol. Yet the provinces did not suddenly impose a total ban on alcohol; rather, new laws amplified the scope of pre-existing regulatory frameworks. Four decades earlier, the North-West Territories Act had banned alcohol in lands largely populated by Native peoples. Historian Gerald Hallowell notes that, before the 1916 Ontario Temperance Act was introduced, close to 600 of its more than 800 municipalities had already voted themselves dry through local options. Furthermore, local governments had already drastically reduced the number of tavern licences. In 1914, fewer than 1,400 licences were issued in Ontario, in contrast to the almost 5,000 issued forty years earlier. Even in Quebec (which was last among the provinces to introduce a prohibition act in 1918, and the first to repeal it a year later), almost half of its municipalities had been dry before the act was imposed. In 1918, the federal government merely capped municipal and provincial regulatory schemes (and its own regulations governing Indians) with an act forbidding the importation, manufacture, or distribution of alcohol within Canada. Thus, for most Canadians, prohibition came more with a whimper than a bang.

In the aftermath of the war, politicians soon realized that strict prohibition would raise the ire of vocal opponents, not the least of whom were soldiers and sailors, who considered a smoke and a pint a fighting man's right. Urbanites, who made up half the Canadian population by 1920, had never been as keen as rural Canadians on outright prohibition. And after the war, calls for the return to normal life included the freedom to drink. After Ottawa lifted national restrictions, the provinces followed, quietly trading outright prohibition for limited tolerance under liquor-licensing regimes.

No such skittishness had accompanied the passage of liquor restrictions among Indians. For status Indians, prohibition was nothing new. Missionaries had long campaigned to prevent whites from selling alcohol to Indians, and to keep Indians from providing them business. Under the Indian Act, persons selling alcohol could be fined or imprisoned, but Indians on reserves were prohibited from making or possessing alcohol. Indian women were subject to further regulation through a subsection prohibiting their presence in saloons. The most coercive clause of the act (and one that never applied to whites) forbade status Indians from being in a 'state of intoxication.' Unscrupulous liquor pedlars, both Canadian and American, none the less bootlegged alcohol onto reserves, caring about nothing but their profits. Missionaries persistently complained to DIA agents and commissioners about the demoralizing effects of alcohol on Native persons whom they were trying to 'civilize.' Drinking undermined the lessons of thrift, hard work, and sexual circumspection that clergymen and industrial-school teachers drummed in. Ironically, the right to drink as other Canadians did provided a more appealing reason for Native people to seek enfranchisement than did the unfulfilled promises of citizenship.

Dire Influences: The Anti-Opium Campaign

Other forms of regulation which did not mention specific ethnic or racial groups nevertheless owed their origins to racist objectives. For instance, white slavery crusaders invariably claimed that 'foreign' men (especially Jews, Italians, and blacks) posed the greatest danger to (white, Christian)

Canadian women. However it was the Opium Act which was most directly connected to Euro-Canadians' fears of a 'foreign' racial group. Notably, the federal government introduced anti-drug legislation without being pressured by religiously inspired lobby groups. Instead, long-standing suspicions about the unassimilability of the Chinese in the idealized biracial nation underwrote a lightning-strike campaign to introduce the nation's first drug laws.

The Chinese were already subjected to the greatest range of regulations imposed on any of Canada's immigrants. Beginning in 1885, once the transcontinental railway was complete, the federal government imposed a $50 head tax through the Chinese Immigration Act. In 1903, the tax jumped to $500, largely in response to pressure from white labour groups and openly racist British Columbian politicians. Wiley employers managed to find ways of manoeuvring around head-tax restrictions, partly by substituting Japanese and East Asian workers for Chinese. When it looked like boatloads were about to flood the B.C. labour market in 1907, the Vancouver Branch of the Asiatic Exclusion League called a protest rally, which degenerated into a riot. A white mob fought its way through Asian sections of the city, smashing every Asian-owned business in its path of rage. Out of this débâcle came an unlikely solution: a bid to impose regulations against the heretofore legal opium industry.

Deputy Minister of Labour (and future prime minister) William Lyon Mackenzie King kick-started a one-man campaign to regulate the consumption of psychoactive drugs. When investigating the losses suffered by Vancouver's Chinese and Japanese businesses, he issued a separate supplementary set of recommendations concerning the opium trade. The use of opium by Chinese labourers was widely known from as early as the 1880s, but it had never before been a target of legal regulation.

King's *Report on the Need for the Suppression of the Opium Traffic in Canada* presented opium as a threat to white Canadians, a claim which resonated with themes played out in white-slavery and temperance crusades. It did not, however, reflect the concerns of the Chinese Anti-Opium Society, a group of social leaders concerned about the drug's effects in their own communities. Instead, King's recommendations attacked Chinese merchants, alleging that they were profiting at the expense of young white men and women who succumbed to the drug's lure. Like white slavery crusaders' tales, his 'evidence' consisted of anecdotes about the 'dire influence' of the opiate and, equally significantly, 'the Chinaman.' Merely three weeks later, his recommendations were translated into the 1908 Opium Act. Anyone who dared to 'import, manufacture, sell or possess for the purposes of selling, opium' faced up to three years in prison, or fines of $1,000. Some exceptions were made: legitimate medical use was permitted, and so was possession and personal use. This law represented an unprecedented form of legal moral regulation, unsupported by a broad reform movement. As legal scholars Robert Solomon and Melvyn Green argue, a whole new category of morals offenders was invented as a result of this law.

Even more than regulations attacking alcohol consumption or commercial sex, the Opium Act focused on specific forms of drug use favoured by a vulnerable minority group. More common forms of psychoactive-drug manufacturing and consumption remained perfectly legal. Notably, opium and morphine were *not* prohibited ingredients in patent medicines sold by druggists and purchased by thousands of Canadians. Chinese manufacturers and distributors of opium, whose operations generated much lower sales than the patent-medicine industry, were clearly to be the prime targets of more heavy-handed regulation. As one senator cynically asked in the brief debate over the Opium Act, 'Would this government have introduced a bill of confiscation such as this if this business had been carried out by white people?' He answered his own question: 'I doubt it very much.' But King and the Liberals did not have to worry about an outcry in defence of Chinese persons' personal liberties or vaunted British justice. By this point, publicity

over the royal commissions and King's grandstanding generated widespread support for the government to regulate
a sphere of life previously untouched by state controls.

Conclusion

From Sunday pleasure outings to saloons, the targets of
moral regulation had multiplied by the early twentieth century. As Protestant lobbyists courted the state in a bid to
bolster the enforcement of moral regulation, they achieved
notable legislative successes. From municipal governments
to Parliament, the state took on a moral-watchdog role.
Still, the legal regulation of non-Native Canadians' morality, while more far-reaching by the end of the First
World War, would never match the controls imposed on
aboriginals.

    But the Indian Act was not the only form of legal regula-
tion which cast its shadow on specific groups of Canadians.
Efforts to combat the alleged white slave trade and to battle
drinking and Sunday amusements were indirect attacks on
working-class and 'foreign' men whose presence in eastern
urban ghettos and in central and western Canadian boom-
towns had become troubling to the Anglo-Canadian majority, and to Protestants in particular. French Quebeckers
were also concerned about the moral character of the increasingly heterogeneous population and the growth in
commercialized cultuure, but there the church maintained
more control than the state over most matters moral. For
rural Quebeckers and devout city-dwellers, the prospect of
family and community disapproval, or sharp words hissed
in confessionals, remained more powerful reminders to
obey moral edicts. For all moral reformers, however, trans-
lating visions of morality into the actual regulation of people, places, and conduct turned out to be less predictable
or satisfying than lobbyists had ever imagined.

4

Incorporating Moral Visions

More ambitious forms of legal moral regulation called for nothing less than new techniques of policing, new courts for the hearing of morals offences, new institutions for the care and control of the immoral, and, above all, the state's commitment to regulate morality uncompromisingly. In several parts of the country, particularly in the biggest cities, many of these changes were instituted by the 1910s. Morality squads, juvenile and women's courts, and a growing roster of reformatories and correctional institutions were established and staffed both by amateur morals monitors and by professionals, including social workers and doctors. Families, communities, and churches continued to exert pressure on individuals to regulate their behaviour, but unprecedented arrest figures for morals offences indicate that the state grew more willing to enforce morality through the law by the early part of the century.

Social purity reformers should have been heartened, but they were a hard lot to please. First, they observed that more rigorous policing nabbed minor offenders, but it failed to snare the big players in organized vice – the white slavers, the drug kingpins, the big-time gamblers and bootleggers. Furthermore, police crack-downs tended to drive vice and immorality underground. This was particularly true in the case of prostitution, which continued to operate on a freelance and pimp-controlled basis after red-light districts were broken up. For every leak plugged by the police, a new one seemed to spring.

Second, neither Protestant nor Catholic moral reformers had ever stopped at wishing for more arrests. As signatories to WCTU pledge cards declared, the ultimate goal of moral regulation was to mould and maintain individual *self*-regulating subjects. If morals offenders were simply arrested, fined, and released, then how could they be taught to regulate themselves? The trouble was that institutionalizing offenders, or hiring professionals to regulate their morality proved to be too expensive and impractical for most jurisdictions to implement; more attractive were fines and licences, both of which options generated revenue. As vice-survey authors persistently complained, these practices merely imposed a tax on vice. They were not far off the mark.

From the point of view of those unlucky individuals who ended up in reformatories, police lock-ups, and psychiatric institutions, social purity advocates need not have worried that legal moral regulation was too lax. By the early twentieth century, state controls over specific groups of morals offenders – juvenile delinquents, prostitutes, vagrants, and homosexuals – were significantly enhanced. And wartime anxieties over Canadians' fitness meant that medical reports of those carrying venereal disease, and the so-called feeble-minded, produced general alarm. Thus, despite municipal and provincial governments' ambivalence about devoting resources and personnel to regulate immorality, authorities remained willing to spend money to incarcerate those deemed to pose the greatest moral threats to Canadian society.

On the Beat: Policing Morality

The Toronto police force had launched the first morality squad in the 1880s, but several other forces followed suit and set up specialized forces devoted to moral regulation by the early twentieth century. Of course, constables (both city officers and Mounted Policemen) continued their traditional duties of arresting disorderly drunks, vagrants, and rambunctious prostitutes. Morality squad officers were meant to be different, however. As undercover detectives, their mandate was to root out vice, and to act on citizens' complaints about immorality in their neighbourhoods, or even in their own families. In cities they concentrated on the 'evils' of prostitution, gambling, and the illegal trade in liquor and drugs. Greg Marquis and John Weaver have noted that the police also intervened in domestic disputes, both by collecting money from deserting husbands and by urging estranged couples to reunite. Their broad mandate cast them as new specialists in state-directed moral regulation. By the 1910s, a handful of women officers joined several city forces as morality squad adjutants, hired at the behest of women's organizations keen to ferret out immorality among young women. Whether investigating suspected brothels, opium dens, 'blind pigs' (illegal bars), or gambling dens, or simply when encountering drunks and streetwalkers on their beats, the men (and a few women) in blue wielded considerable discretionary power. Lucky morals offenders might escape with a lecture, but officers could escort the unlucky to jail.

The altered character of policing at the turn of the century clearly shows that haranguing could work. In effect, the police were policed as never before. Organizations such as the Toronto Vigilance Committee, a kind of evangelical vigilante group, shadowed the local force's every move, pouncing upon the slightest hint of evidence that officers winked at vice or, more shocking still, profited from it. Montreal's Committee of Sixteen was a Protestant-dominated coalition of medical professionals and philanthropists, organized in 1918 to rescue the city from its reputation as 'a spectacle of triumphant vice.' When public-relations problems became critical, forces across the country adopted new tactics and adapted to changes demanded by critics. In Vancouver, for instance, the B.C. government placed the local police under the control of an independent police commission in 1904 after the city force had refused to stamp out prostitution. When social purity reformers raised charges of corruption, denials were made, but their allegations of laxity stuck. In smaller towns, police chiefs excused their shortcomings by pointing to their limited budgets; in big cities, police forces cracked down on women and men involved in the sex trade, arresting hundreds when they normally had arrested handfuls, all to appease meddlesome citizens.

According to John McLaren, national criminal court statistics show that the white slavery panic, and the ensuing pressure from social purity groups to clamp down on organized vice, prompted repeated police sweeps of brothels in vice districts, not only in puritanical cities such as Toronto, but in the smaller, formerly looser cities of Calgary, Edmonton, and Vancouver. The annual rate of convictions for bawdy-house offences (being an inmate or keeper thereof) skyrocketed, from approximately 2,800 in 1910 to close to 5,500 by 1915. Even more striking was the conviction rate of almost 90 per cent.

Arrests spiked at the height of reform agitation. Although Winnipeg was the only large city which openly cordoned off vice, local moral reformers were quick to point to the tacit toleration that prevailed in most cities. Even in Montreal, which enjoyed a dubious reputation as a European-style 'open city,' brothel arrests rose steadily in the early 1910s: they shot up from slightly more than 1,000 in 1914, to almost 3,000 in 1918, the year the Committee of Sixteen released its critical vice report. Public criticism produced similar results in Toronto after Reverend R.B. St Clair of the Toronto Vigilance Committee vocally attacked the police force's tolerance and unwillingness to carry out the law. As a result, the number of arrests for 'being found in a house of ill fame' jumped from slightly more than 100 in 1912 (the year of the Vigilance Committee's attack) to a staggering 674 arrests the following year.

Yet, for a variety of reasons, prostitution itself was still not eliminated. Police rarely subjected men to the same sanctions imposed on female prostitutes, even though statutes permitted them to charge men with 'keeping' or 'being found in' a brothel, 'procuring,' or 'living off the avails of prostitution' (which, taken together, would have comprised the substantial majority of persons involved in prostitution if police forces had enforced the laws equitably). Instead, the war on white slavery and the campaign against organized vice were fought overwhelmingly at the expense of prostitutes and brothel-keepers. For example, over the period from 1912 to 1917, Vancouver police finally responded to years of criticism by attacking prostitution, especially in the city's Chinatown, where prostitutes, gamblers, and petty crooks had long congregated, despite the objections of respectable Chinese businessmen. But police records show that arrests of women involved in the sex trade vastly outnumbered those of men, even if prostitutes are eliminated from the total. While 332 women were charged with keeping houses of ill fame over this five-year period (compared with 29 men), a mere 7 men were arrested for living off the avails of prostitution (meaning pimping). Of these 7 men, only 2 were convicted and given prison terms of six months each – hardly a disincentive for men who saw an opportunity to profit from concerted campaigns to shut down madam-operated brothels. If social purity advocates had hoped to make male customers and exploiters of women pay for their sins, the enforcement of prostitution legislation was a flop. Thanks to the anti-brothel campaigns which rocked Canadian cities in the 1910s, the red lights that had burned in every town and city in the nation in the 1890s had been dimmed by the end of the First World War, reducing the visible presence of commercial sex. However, they continued to flicker in other forms and locations.

This was where female police officers came into the picture, as Tamara Myers has argued. Volunteers associated with Local Councils of Women and the WCTU had been acting as *de facto* undercover cops for years, patrolling train stations and docks, on the lookout for potential white slavers and their quarry. As the original Travellers' Aid ladies, YWCA women became amateur surveillance officers who claimed that they could tell in a glance whether a young woman was *in* trouble, or *looking* for it. Leading clubwomen came up with a radical idea: Why not offer their special skills to police? Over the 1910s they did just that, and police chiefs in Kingston, Ottawa, Winnipeg, London, Montreal, Vancouver, Toronto, St Thomas, and Halifax listened. With the support of the francophone Fédération Nationale Saint-Jean-Baptiste, the chair of the Montreal Local Council of Women, Katherine Chipman, managed to convince parsimonious municipal politicians that women officers could turn urban moral-danger zones, such as parks and commercial leisure areas, into their 'beats.' In practice, female members of morality squads maintained their informal scrutiny of activities favoured by young, working-class women. Although their professional status within police forces was shaky, they blazed the trail for a style of policing which blended protection and coercion. Women officers patrolled train stations, movie houses, cheap theatres, and parks to monitor their erring sisters. Their efforts were not well received by the masculine policing establishment, however, and, as a result, women officers' influence in city policing declined after the war, as enthusiasm for anti-vice advocacy generally waned. The entry of women into professional police forces and their search for *potential* criminal acts nevertheless symbolized an important shift in the character of legal moral regulation, from the traditional reactive approach in favour of one which anticipated and sanctioned predicted moral lapses.

Regulating Desires: Homosexuality and Heterosexuality

Prostitution was not the only form of illicit sexuality to receive unprecedented attention at the turn of the century. The Criminal Code provided a flexible means for police forces to regulate sexual desires, both heterosexual and homosexual. The police had long relied on the broadly defined charge of vagrancy to suppress commercialized sex, but had used this tool only against suspected prostitutes. Although heterosexual male customers were never a policing priority, urban police forces became increasingly concerned with homosexuals. Thus it was not merely heterosexual vice which commanded police attention in the early years of the twentieth century, but a broad spectrum of stigmatized sexual desires.

The regulation of morally suspect desires never amounted to complete suppression; rather, it meant that certain types of people, found in certain places, at certain times, were subjected to legal penalties. Disapproval of homosexuality has a long and notorious past, rooted in canon (church) law, which defined sodomy as an 'abominable' and 'unnatural' act, contrary to God's law. In Canada, homosexual acts, as well as bestiality, had been considered sins, and they eventually fell under the legal category of 'offences against public morals.' In the late nineteenth century, penalties for homosexual contact were reduced, but the range of acts for which men could be arrested expanded with the introduction in 1890 of a new offence: 'gross indecency,' a crime which carried a maximum charge of five years, along with the lash. So 'gross' was this offence that legislators could not bring themselves to describe precisely what it meant. Fuzzy legal definitions did not impede police from acting, since they proceeded to arrest men engaged in almost any form of close physical intimacy.

Because the policing of sexual activities depended on surveillance, the implementation of homosexual regulation varied considerably, between town and country, and between different provinces. Raiding brothels in established red-light districts was like shooting fish in a barrel compared with catching men 'in flagrante delicto.' Terry Chapman's research shows that, in rural areas and small towns, amateur spies played a critical role in bringing homosexual activities to the attention of Mounties or local constables. For instance, two boys who peeked through a window and witnessed a Regina dry-goods merchant engaged in sex acts with two other men tipped off the territorial police in 1895. Farmers and livestock workers who thought they could steal a private moment behind a barn or in a patch of tall grass were sometimes startled by observers, who could turn them over to the authorities if they felt so inclined. The fact that men (and boys, in some cases) sought out darkened or hidden spaces for their sexual activities indicates that community regulation – the anticipated disapproval of church, family, neighbours, and co-workers – remained a powerful force in the regulation of desire. In rural areas especially, the state's coercive powers were invoked only after traditional forms of regulation broke down.

In urban Canada, particularly in cities which boasted detective or morality squads, police officers were more directly involved in regulating homosexuality. In cases involving assaults on young boys, parents and boys themselves raised a hue and cry, but the bulk of arrestees appear to have been engaged in consensual sex. This pattern of law enforcement was directly attributable to new forms of policing which bordered on entrapment, according to Steven Maynard. The Toronto police force was the nation's leader in tailoring surveillance techniques to catch men having sex. Not content to cast light in dark alleys where men sometimes engaged in sex acts, the force set up undercover observation posts in the city's public washrooms, where officers attached to the Morality Department squinted at men through holes in cubicle partitions. Maynard recounts a 1919 incident, in which two constables hiding in a Queen's Park lavatory at night spied on three men engaged in mutual masturbation. Satisfied that they were committing an act of gross indecency, one policemen burst on the scene with his flashlight, while the other dutifully jotted in his notebook that the men had their penises out. In a familiar pattern, such heroic efforts did not eradicate homosexuality, just as red-light-district sweeps failed to stop prostitution. Men who could afford hotel rooms, or who entertained other men in the privacy of their own homes, were rarely arrested in this period. And although the risk of arrest certainly increased in the early twentieth century, men continued to gravitate to alleyways, public lavatories, and park bushes in the hope of encountering men with similar desires.

Heterosexual desire also fell under stricter legal constraints in this period of nation-building, but not because it was considered unnatural or abominable. The crusade against organized prostitution was accompanied by a collateral campaign to stamp out casual heterosexual encounters, particularly among young people. Sabbatarians in organizations such as the Lords' Day Alliance had highlighted the conflict between proper recreation and immoral entertainment. One spin-off of that movement was increased attention to the dubious pastimes of youth. Both rural dwellers and urbanites worried that young people were ill equipped to make the proper moral choices necessary to send them on their way to marriage and family life. On the one hand, there were church suppers, fraternal-order meetings, and sewing or barn-raising bees; on the other, commercial amusements, including circuses, nickelodeons, dancehalls, and burlesque theatres – all of which depended on and encouraged heterosexual familiarity. Historian Lynne Marks suggests that rural couples who engaged in trysts may have faced less regulation than their urban counterparts (who, after all, would suspect that a buggy-ride home from church was really an excuse to have sex?). But because Canadians believed that vice found its home in cities, not the pristine countryside, legal forms of regulation on heterosexual activities emerged first and most visibly in the country's biggest cities.

The elastic definition of vagrancy provided a handy device for heterosexual regulation. For men, it implied a state of joblessness or shiftlessness; for women, especially young women, it referred to sexual immorality. Typically an officer would encounter a woman alone on the street at night. As the wrong kind of person in the wrong place at the wrong of time of day, she was immediately suspect. If she failed to supply a convincing explanation for her presence, she would be arrested and, in all likelihood, convicted, since vagrancy could be tried summarily in magistrate's court. In most cases rowdy or lewd behaviour attracted police attention, but the statute none the less allowed officers the discretion to arrest anyone whom they suspected of being promiscuous. Predictably, it was during the height of the social purity movement's pressure on the police that vagrancy charges for women rose markedly.

Proscribing Pleasures: Alcohol and Drugs

Promiscuity or curb-crawling did not leave heterosexual men vulnerable to arrest, so long as they were not downright abusive or disorderly in the process. But that did not mean that they were free to pursue any pastime, particularly if they were young, foreign, and/or working-class. During the white slavery panic, hundreds were arrested and fined for being 'frequenters' of brothels. However, men's desires for a quick drink or a fast buck were more likely to attract the attention of police officers. Just as working-class women and prostitutes bore the brunt of policing that criminalized heterosexual expressiveness, so the enforcement of drinking, gambling, and drug laws fell most heavily on the shoulders of 'foreigners' and men of all ethnicities involved in public cultures of working-class masculinity.

Prohibition laws in action illustrate how morals policing tends to stigmatize status, rather than sanction immoral behaviour *per se.* A lack of effective enforcement mechanisms hampered alcohol restrictions from the start. Whenever localities were voted 'dry,' or provincial acts restricted the consumption of alcohol, illegal stills and blind pigs were sure to sprout. Since police officers and Mounties lacked the resources to root out every illegal supplier and consumer of alcohol, arrests of violators were never more than token attempts to demonstrate the state's seriousness about temperance. In cities such as Halifax, with its steady supply of thirsty sailors, the police were content to target only the rowdiest blind pigs. 'Foreign' men who produced cheap alcohol from every manner of grain, vegetable, and fruit were more vulnerable to arrest than were Anglo-Canadian men who could discretely visit their physicians for 'prescription' intoxicants. James Gray notes that newspapers invariably mentioned arrestees' ethnicity when they reported police raids, thereby fixing race as a critical marker of morality. One report in the *Moose Jaw Times* put the matter bluntly: 'Among the [Anglo-] Canadians there are many who do not drink at all. Among the French there are very few who do not drink. Among the Germans and Half-breeds there are absolutely none at all.'

Loopholes in prohibition statutes, particularly the allowance of interprovincial trade prior to the 1918 federal act, led to a version of moral regulation not unlike musical chairs: province A might allow the export of alcohol; prospective customers in province B might drink the grog, or they might resell it to clients in province C. Gray mentions that border towns, such as Kenora and Hull, profited handsomely by supplying drinkers in the neighbouring provinces of Manitoba and Ontario with wine, beer, or spirits. If consumers found interprovincial travel too arduous, they could order by mail. Since prohibition acts of the 1910s did not ban alcohol advertising, it was as easy to order a case of whisky as it was to order a pair of trousers from the Eaton's catalogue.

None the less, provincially regulated prohibition did reduce arrests for drunkenness. In Saskatchewan, the number dropped from almost 3,000 in 1913 (just before the province's prohibition act) to slightly more than 400 by 1918. In Alberta, more than 7,000 arrests were made in 1913, but only 391 in 1917. Undoubtedly the absence of young men, off to fight the war, accounted for a large measure of this decline, but temperance advocates were happy to attribute the change to legislation wisely adopted by the state.

Despite the fiscal belt-tightening in the Indian Affairs department after 1896, federal money was still set aside to enforce the special liquor regulations for status Indians. The Indian Act explicitly prohibited alcohol from reserves, but drunkenness and rowdiness were frequent weekend occurrences. Whites and non-status Indians violated the act's spatial and racial regulations by smuggling liquor to customers on reserves. Disputes also arose within reserves, between those converted to Christianity (and pledged to abstinence) and those who rejected clergymen's moralizing. So flagrantly were liquor restrictions flouted that in 1913 the department ordered Indian agents across the country to step up their policing of sexual vice, immorality, and drinking. Agents could impose fines or prison terms for liquor offences virtually on the spot. And, of course, status Indians remained the only persons who could be punished merely for being drunk, whether or not they were causing trouble.

Ethnic and class biases also emerged in the enforcement of federal drug laws. Between 1912 and 1920, prosecutions under these newly minted restrictions produced more than 900 convictions per year in Canada. Not surprisingly, the provinces with the biggest Chinatowns (Quebec, Ontario, and British Columbia) produced the highest numbers of arrests. Fears of black 'dope fiends' also influenced policing patterns, particularly in U.S. border cities such as Windsor. From 1912 to 1920, Chinese and black offenders together comprised two-thirds of those sentenced in the province's major cities. The fact that courts issued fines rather than jail terms in 90 per cent of cases was clearly an incentive for police to make arrests. For the white officers, who were legally eligible to receive half the fines imposed on offenders, and for the municipal and provincial coffers, which grew richer thanks to convictions, legal regulations intended to stem the desire for certain drugs provided new sources of revenue. Simultaneously, drug-law enforcement ensured that black-market prices would continue to climb.

Despite repeated evidence that proscribing pleasures (particularly addictive ones) tended to backfire, both alcohol prohibition and drug laws were retained and revamped after the war. Rural-based prohibition forces had been swept aside by urban voters, and women had not voted in numbers sufficiently large or as solidly pro-prohibition as lobbyists had hoped. By establishing provincial liquor boards as a compromise, a policy most provinces adopted by the late 1920s, governments came up with a novel solution: they would now regulate alcohol consumption by tolerating it, under certain circumstances. For instance, statutes defined acceptable levels of alcohol in drinks; dictated where, when, and how much alcohol could be consumed; and determined who could consume alcohol (largely non-Native men) and who could not (minors; status Indians; and, in some public venues, women). Liquor licensing, unlike prohibition, was a cash cow, for state regulatory schemes absorbed the enormous profits that bootleggers had been pocketing. Drug prohibitions, in contrast, were maintained and reinforced as anti-Asian racism peaked in the mid-1920s. In any case, drug-taking, boozing, and prostitution did not cease once these new morals laws came into effect.

Moral Menaces and Medico-Legal Regulation: VD and 'Feeble-Mindedness'

As social purity advocates chided, citizens who drank, gambled, smoked opium, or frequented bawdy-houses failed to measure up to ideal standards of citizenship. Equally troubling, especially in wartime, were those who threatened to corrupt otherwise strong, pure Canadians. Medical experts and social commentators labelled as 'the unfit' those who were chronically unemployed, mentally subnormal, and/or heterosexually hyperactive. People who carried venereal diseases were pictured as walking time bombs in medical reports which revealed alarmingly high rates of infection among recruits to the Canadian Expeditionary Force. As Mary Louise Adams and Jennifer Stephen have argued, a hybrid form of medico-legal regulation emerged by the 1910s to combat these problems. In the process, voluntary agencies, medical professionals, and clinics were linked to pre-established institutions of social control (prisons and reformatories), as well as to new women's and juvenile courts.

One of the perennial subthemes in debates over prostitution was the spread of venereal diseases. Historically, state schemes for VD control, such as the English Contagious Diseases Acts, had attempted to protect male customers from infection by subjecting prostitutes to compulsory medical exams and treatments. A less coercive (and more effective) means of fighting sexually transmitted diseases would have been to allow the manufacture and sale of condoms, but this was not to be in Canada. Section 179 of the Criminal Code made it illegal to 'sell, advertise, publish an advertisement of ... any medicine, drug, or article intended or represented as a means of preventing conception or causing abortion.' On the one hand, this legal regulation reinforced cultural expectations that sex occurred only within marriage for the purpose of procreation; on the other, it made the transmission of sexual diseases more likely. Over the 1910s new medico-legal regulations were introduced to police VD sufferers and suspected carriers – now including men. Although medical support for birth control would become more vocal and acceptable in the 1930s, the regulatory mechanisms imposed on infected persons and the so-called unfit remained in place.

Squeamishness over speaking too explicitly about sex muffled public discussion of syphilis and gonorrhoea prior to the war. Once Canadians learned that one in six of

Canada's overseas soldiers was infected, military and medical authorities declared a national emergency, as Jay Cassel shows. How had the men become infected? While some Canadians conveniently blamed English and French camp-followers, military brass countered that troops had become infected by Canadian women *prior* to enlistment. Military investigations revealed that the disease was most prevalent among recruits based in Halifax, Quebec, Montreal, Kingston, Toronto, and London. Since that was the case, civic leaders resolved that the war against sexual vice would have to be fought on the home front as well as in Europe. In 1917 the federal government took action by making it illegal for any woman suffering from venereal disease to have sexual intercourse, or to invite or solicit intercourse, with any member of His Majesty's forces. Women suspected of being infected could be charged under the law and incarcerated for one week, pending the results of medical tests. This was not simply a matter of protecting individual soldiers: it was a component of the wartime 'Defence of Canada Order.'

Defending Canada from venereal disease meant forcing male soldiers to undergo treatment, but it also meant subjecting women, particularly poor women who could not afford private medical care, to unprecedented forms of moral regulation. Historians Suzanne Buckley and Janice Dickin (McGinnis) argue that Canadian feminists did not object to the gender and class biases of VD control since they felt that military regulations swept up women who were already 'a disgrace to the feminine sex.' Restraints on the sexual exploits of promiscuous women were rationalized as a necessary means of protecting the 'fit' from the 'unfit.'

In its familiar role as the nation's leader in regulating morality through law, Ontario was the first province to link medical and legal controls over suspected carriers of venereal disease. The first move came in 1909 with the establishment of a psychiatric out-patient clinic attached to the Toronto General Hospital. Jennifer Stephen's research shows that the leading psychiatric experts of the day surveyed patients, usually referred by criminal courts or social workers, in order to determine if illicit sexuality, venereal disease, and 'feeble-mindedness' were linked. Once diagnosed, they could be incarcerated, either in the Mercer Reformatory or in the Orillia Asylum for the Insane. Both men and women were sent to the clinic, but medical personnel were more interested in their female charges on account of their allegedly alarming capacity to reproduce. In a 1917 report titled *The Prevalence of Venereal Diseases in Canada*, clinic head Dr C.K. Clarke claimed that 60 per cent of prostitutes were 'feeble-minded,' and that 'prostitutes are the source from which the greater part of the infections come.' Confident in his assessments, he added: 'carefully compiled statistics show that 75 per cent [of VD cases] are traceable to the women of the street.'

What did it take to be labelled 'feeble-minded'? Clinical reports show that this diagnosis was typically based on evidence that women drifted from job to job, had illegitimate children, or had multiple sexual partners. A typical case file read as follows: 'L. is an occupational wanderer, having worked in candy factories, restaurants, etc. Has venereal disease. Has been immoral with two or three boys – would go to a park. Charged with not reporting for treatment. Is a mental defective.' Such expert assessments sounded remarkably similar to the notes untrained policewomen took on their patrols. Indeed, women often ended up in the clinic after being picked up for vagrancy. In spite of psychiatrists' expertise, their diagnoses of feeblemindedness owed more to their opinions about moral lapses than to disinterested evaluations of intellectual abilities.

The wartime panic over venereal disease pushed the state to widen the net cast over those suspected, for one reason or another, of being unfit. In 1918, the Ontario Royal Commission on Venereal Disease and Feeble-Mindedness recommended the establishment of free treatment clinics and the imposition of fines for those who refused treatment. Ontario, New Brunswick, Saskatchewan, and British Columbia all put such measures into law. More important, these new regulations and the relentless public campaigns about the dangers posed by the unfit lent legitimacy to the diagnosis and forced medical treatment of women and men suffering from venereal disease and/or labelled as feeble-minded.

Order in the Courts: Children and Women

Many of the girls and women who ended up in VD clinics were ordered there by courts. While men continued to appear before justices of the peace or in police magistrates' courts, a handful of cities introduced separate courts in the 1910s to try cases involving women and children. Women's courts were designed to shield female morals offenders and victims from low-minded spectators. Juvenile courts tried young people not only separately, but also differently, under the 1908 Juvenile Delinquents Act (JDA). Thus women and children became the first cohorts to experience what Dorothy Chunn has called 'socialized justice,' in which non-legal actors lent a hand to care for, and not just to punish, offenders.

Instituting a parallel system of justice for juveniles was the child-welfare movement's *pièce de résistance*. In 1908 Children's Aid Society (CAS) leaders successfully lobbied the federal government to pass the JDA to deal with cases involving juveniles in danger or in conflict with the law. With the exception of the 1876 consolidated Indian Act, it was the first statute to prescribe a distinct style of justice for a subgroup of Canadians. Since neither Euro-Canadian children nor Indians were considered to be fully rational or responsible, they were exposed to legal regulations designed to protect and control. Of course, specialized justice, like the reserve system, was costly. But CAS leaders had a compelling argument: spend a few pennies now for the treatment of youth, or pay dearly later – in stolen property, broken lives, and expensive prison bills.

At the same time the JDA also invented new ways for juveniles (and their parents) to be defined as morals offenders. Children could be charged with ill-defined offences which, if committed by adults, did not amount to criminal acts. Consequently, youngsters faced the possibility of ending up in juvenile court for 'incorrigibility,' being 'beyond parental control,' and 'delinquency.' Courts were empowered to remove youth to foster homes, place them under CAS supervision, or sentence them to indefinite periods of incarceration in juvenile detention. Under the JDA, adults could also be convicted of 'contributing to the delinquency of a minor.' Like many laws governing morality, this offence was vague enough to allow court officers flexibility in applying the law to protect children. As a summary section of the act declared, the scope of juvenile-court powers was meant to be interpreted liberally, so that 'the care and custody and discipline of a juvenile delinquent shall approximate as nearly as may be that which should be given by its parents.'

The JDA also symbolized the state's growing inclination to enlist non-state actors to regulate morality. For example, CAS officers, already quasi-parental figures, became probation officers attached to juvenile courts, despite their lack of formal legal or professional training. Probation officers were to play a critical role in the administration of the courts, for they were to prepare reports on every offender, and to divert as many as possible from prison. Other extralegal actors, such as the Big Brothers and Big Sisters, gradually assumed authority to supervise male and female youth serving probation orders. Family members were also added to the mix, since parents were often required to attend hearings and to vouch for their children's supervision on probation. The result was a semi-formal version of adjudication. One contemporary legal commentator declared that juvenile courts were really 'social clinics.' Yet juvenile courts remained part of the criminal justice system: the threat of incarceration and punishment remained.

This double-edged philosophy of moral regulation also operated in women's courts. Like the movement to introduce women police officers, the push for women's courts was backed by women's organizations, including the National Council of Women and the YWCA. Advocates anticipated that separate women's courts, with the public excluded, would allow magistrates to distinguish between innocent victims, such as women inveigled into prostitution, and evil-minded women bent on corrupting the impressionable. Women's-court lobbyists did not plan to offer women offenders tickets to freedom; rather they hoped that separate courts would permit female court visitors and probation officers to care for unfortunate women, while leaving those 'hardened in sin' in the hands of the state penal system. In 1913, Toronto sponsored the country's first women's court, and several other large cities followed. Although no more than a score of women's and juvenile courts were established in Canada by the War's end, they signalled that the movement for socialized justice had been launched – beginning with women and children, the guinea pigs in an emergent welfarist approach to criminal justice.

Conclusion

The capacity of the state to impose regulatory schemes was enormously enhanced over the late nineteenth and early-twentieth centuries. Yet practical limitations and conflicting interpretations of policy undermined the scope and intensity of surveillance and control. One wrinkle in the smooth development of regulatory regimes was regional variation. Not all provinces shared the enthusiasm for the legal regulation of morality. Another was cost: new institutions, like reformatories, were expensive, and the professionals who staffed them – not just prison guards and matrons but social workers, doctors, probation officers, and psychiatrists – expected to be paid salaries. Still another was practical: where were municipal and provincial authorities supposed to incarcerate all of these prostitutes, drunks, opium-smokers, and VD carriers? One solution, common on the prairies, was to arrest minor morals offenders (especially prostitutes), but to order them quietly to leave town. Not surprisingly, poorer provinces were much slower to develop the full range of strategies to contain the immoral. Within provinces, rural areas were less well served than cities by state custodial institutions. As a result, traditional forms of familial and communal regulation ruled in these regions long after big cities, such as Vancouver and Montreal, had built separate institutions for the custody of women, men, and children.

Culture and religion also complicated the picture. Catholics and Protestants bickered over the best means to correct deviant behaviour. For serious offenders, who were sent to federal penitentiaries, separate religious services and instruction were offered. However, minor offenders, particularly juveniles, were confined in institutions segregated by sect. In Quebec, and in provinces such as Manitoba, where the concentration of French Catholics was high, religious orders housed and monitored minor offenders in exchange for per-capita operating grants. In spite of non denominational social workers' growing influence in criminal justice circles, turn-of-the-century corrections continued to resonate with religious notions of care.

For all the effort that went in to them, regulatory schemes, once implemented, rarely yielded expected results. Law reformers had hoped to net the big fish, but institutions of social control ended up catching the small fry – juveniles, petty morals offenders, and vagrants. Few men were ever arrested for procuring, whereas juveniles, who were supposed to have been diverted from the criminal justice system under the JDA, actually faced higher risks of incarceration *after* juvenile courts were established. Adult morals offenders who were convicted usually paid for their offences in fines, not time in correctional settings. Anti-vice campaigners thought that legal regulations were all-purpose tools, capable of fixing any social problem; police forces and politicians saw morals laws as containment devices prone to leaking and spilling over. However mixed the results and limited the success of legal moral regulation in the early twentieth century, governments regulated an even-wider range of moral problems in the postwar era.

PART III: WIDENING THE NET, 1919–1939

5

Returning to Normalcy

'Our boys fought in one great war in France against the mailed fist to keep Canada free. May I not enlist you as soldiers in this new Great War against disease to make and keep Canada clean?' Thus the Honourable Mr Justice Riddell, president of the Canadian Social Hygiene Council (CSHC), concluded his 1927 speech on the council's mission to promote Canadians' health and happiness. By this time the panic over venereal diseases had subsided, however. In the 1920s, the treatment of syphilis and gonorrhoea became a responsibility of the federal Health department, an agency which had not even existed prior to the war. Riddell and his colleagues could congratulate themselves on having extended the regulatory reach of the national government, over matters not only of public health, but of education and welfare.

In the aftermath of war, politicians and moral-reform advocates grew more confident that the state could and *should* extend its control over civilian life for the moral good of the nation. Mobilizing public support to fight the war had tapped resources on the home front no less than on the front lines. Yet many regulations introduced 'for the duration,' such as alcohol prohibitions and amusement taxes, were maintained after the fighting ended.

In this chapter we turn to several important fields in which legal forms of regulation were invented, enhanced, or modified in the postwar period. Three themes – marriage, the family, and citizenship – stand out as key components of the postwar project to reaffirm what it meant to be Canadian. In turn, novel approaches to state moral regulation emerged. By the 1920s, licensing and fining overtook incarceration as the principal legal means of morals regulation. Ironically, policing morality became profitable because people continued to violate moral regulations. Indeed, without the money generated by regulatory agencies such as provincial liquor commissions, the provinces would have found it difficult to fund social welfare schemes, such as compulsory schooling.

The Married State

Making and keeping Canada 'clean' meant much more than protecting people from disease. For this reason the CSHC had changed its name from the National Council for Combatting Venereal Diseases in 1921. Social hygiene was a much broader concept, one which incorporated ideals of patriotic citizenship, vigorous health, and proper attitudes towards sex and marriage. More than 60,000 young men had perished in the killing fields, drastically reducing the stock of fit Canadians. Ensuring the survival of 'the coming generation' became a critical project led by a new crop of child-welfare experts, social workers, and doctors. The introduction of mothers' allowances and an increased effort to force fathers to maintain their wives and children are two examples of a new commitment to protect widows and their children. Minimum-wage laws for specified female workers (in every province but Prince Edward Island) were passed with similar objectives regarding young, wage-earning women's health. But state assistance came with strings attached. Support was provided to encourage marriage, fit child-bearing, acceptable child-rearing practices, and, above all, the heterosexual nuclear family. Anything which threatened these ideals – divorce, birth control, the propagation of the 'unfit' – continued to inspire grave concerns.

Wartime absences had not necessarily made hearts grow fonder. Indeed, some went stone cold as marriage partners discovered that they were happier apart, or with other partners, than with their spouses. According to historian James Snell, the expense and publicity involved in obtaining a parliamentary divorce decree (the legal requirement for divorce in most provinces) did not keep the annual divorce rate from rising quickly – from about 50 divorces per year in the pre-war decade to approximately 600 by the mid-1920s.

Politicians, religious leaders, and civil law reformers considered two regulatory responses to marital disharmony: allowing easier access to legal divorce, or revising provincial laws to impose tighter restrictions on marriage. While the federal government ducked the issue, the provinces (which held jurisdiction over family law) were more willing to move in the latter direction than in the former. Since marriage is a means of regulating sexuality and reproduction, only a small group of liberal divorce advocates risked advocating legal reforms which threatened to hoist such a fundamental moral anchor. Of course, marriage laws could not (and *did* not) prevent members of unhappy couples from deserting, committing adultery or bigamy, or failing to provide the necessities of life. Such calamities might occur, especially in the aftermath of war, but the state was unwilling to encourage them, as a Nova Scotia judge proclaimed in a 1926 divorce trial: 'the Court must keep in mind that marriage is a basic and essential part of the social system, and that its duty is to uphold the married state ...' Perhaps unconscious of his pun, Judge Graham neatly articulated the vital connection between the state of the nation and marriage.

The legal governance of marriage was clearly connected to gender regulation. Husbands were to be breadwinners and wives who had made wartime cameo appearances as munitions workers and tram drivers were to be homemakers. If authorities expected men to forswear their bachelor habits and soldiers' lifestyles to provide a stable home, they deemed women responsible for making their husbands' homes happy. Accordingly, wives were more likely to be held accountable when discord arose, and working outside the home for pay was a sure way to attract censure. These marital norms were not so much expressions of a male 'conspiracy' to keep women down as indications of the importance of marriage as a symbol of social order otherwise shaken by the war and sorely tested during the Depression. Heterosexual marriage, in short, was a way to demonstrate that life *in general* remained normal, as a Vancouver educator stated: 'men should behave like men and women should behave like women.'

Religious, familial, and community censure of married women and men who 'misbehaved' remained powerful disincentives to marriage breakdown, but the state also expanded its regulation of marital morality. One example of this effort was the institution of spousal maintenance acts, implemented in every province except Quebec by 1941. British Columbia's Testators' Family Maintenance Act of 1920 established that not even death could keep the state from reaching into a man's pockets! On the surface, these acts were directed at irresponsible husbands who shirked their duty to support their dependants; indirectly, maintenance laws also regulated married women's morality, in that wives' eligibility to petition the courts for maintenance orders depended on their sexual respectability. Dennis Guest notes that women who themselves had deserted for any reason (including, in provinces other than Ontario, cruel treatment) were ineligible, as were those who had committed adultery, even if they had been deserted. Maintenance acts legally reinforced married women's economic dependency and men's economic responsibilities, and simultaneously upheld the normative vision of gender within marriage.

Maintaining marriage in the postwar era increasingly involved professional regulators. Morality-squad police officers, church workers, and family members had traditionally helped to track down husbands on behalf of deserted wives, but state-sanctioned social welfare agencies which had emerged at the turn of the century assumed greater responsibilities in the interwar period. In Montreal, for instance, Catholic husbands who left their wives could expect a visit from the parish priest, or the Catholic Children's Aid Society, while Protestants might encounter representatives from the Family Welfare Association or the Society for the Protection of Women and Children. These agents, like CAS workers, were empowered to act as special constables of the provincial police. Dorothy Chunn argues that, in provinces where juvenile courts were established, adults could be punished as contributors to delinquency if investigators uncovered evidence of parental adultery. Thus both the criminal and civil law were employed in the struggle to keep families 'normal.'

Yet marriage regulators were not omnipotent. Husbands who failed to support their wives and children usually failed to provide forwarding addresses. Tracing men who had left town, let alone the country, heavily taxed social agencies' time and energy, particularly during the Depression, when desertion rates skyrocketed. Moreover, catching a shirker did not guarantee that he would pay, especially if he was destitute himself. And jailing him for non-support not only did the wife little good, but cost the state money. Considering these obstacles against effective enforcement, social welfare agents' commitment to seemingly futile maintenance statutes seems curious. But abandoning them would have suggested that the state had forsaken its commitment to regulate normative marital roles – the bedrock of civil society.

Parallel legislation restricted access to marriage. These two seemingly contradictory efforts – narrowing the entrance to marriage while barring the exit – were actually complementary, for it was commonly thought that inadequate preparation for marriage was a leading cause of marital breakdown. It was 'entered into by girls of tender years, without realizing what is before them ...,' the Social Welfare Commission of Winnipeg reflected. But psychological preparation alone was considered insufficient, since restocking 'the race' was critical to postwar social stability. Fears that feeble-minded, venereal disease–carrying persons might marry and propagate the *wrong* kind of citizens prompted Alberta, Saskatchewan, and British Columbia to pass legislation requiring prospective spouses to pass VD tests before being granted a marriage licence. Although other provinces were less willing to regulate marriage through medical inspections, every province save Quebec became pickier when it came to sanctioning marriage and child-bearing. Stricter licensing provisions, mandated 'cooling-off periods,' and tougher requirements regarding parental consent were introduced to ensure that only the fit and proper would take on the project of raising the 'coming generation.'

All in the Family

The ideal family was critical to the creation of new citizens, but child-welfare workers amassed considerable evidence in the pre-war years to show that many families, particularly in poor and aboriginal communities, fell short of the ideals expounded by self-appointed welfare experts. One organization, the Canadian Council on Child Welfare (CCCW), became a powerful voice in debates over the management of family life. As it expanded its mandate, the CCCW changed its name to the Canadian Council on Child *and Family* Welfare in 1929, and, more broadly still, to the Canadian Welfare Council in 1937. Headed by Charlotte Whitton, a political dynamo, it expressly declared that regulating family life was the most important means of passing on British values and ensuring the 'purity' of the (Anglo-Celtic) race. 'Family life is the cornerstone of our national life,' Whitton pronounced in 1936: 'British people have carried with them everywhere this basic characteristic.' As historians Patricia Rooke and Rudy Schnell note, French Catholics were not impressed with Whitton's brand of fam-

ily welfare lobbying, and family regulation in Quebec remained more firmly under the yoke of the church than it
was elsewhere in Canada.

A direct product of the child-welfare movement was the
formation in 1929 of Canada's first 'Domestic Relations'
court in Toronto. Although Montreal was the only other
city outside Ontario which established a similar court in the
interwar period, Toronto's (and later Hamilton's and Ottawa's) foreshadowed a movement towards fully fledged family justice. In Toronto, the juvenile court and women's
court (with Dr Margaret Patterson presiding after 1922)
laid the way for a new court which would treat all matters
relating to the regulation of families in one overarching
setting. The court had jurisdiction over the provincial Children's Protection Act, the Deserted Wives' and Children's
Maintenance Act, the Children of Unmarried Parents Act,
and the federal Juvenile Delinquency Act. It was also empowered to preside over matters involving violations of
criminal statutes prohibiting assault, vagrancy, and non-
support.

The court made collecting support payments from male
breadwinners one of its principal activities, thereby materi-
ally aiding women and children in distress, particularly
during the Depression. Monies collected in 1930 amounted
to close to $180,000, compared with less than $23,000 in
1928, a year before the court's formation. However, such
success required court officers to enhance their supervision
of poor families, as Dorothy Chunn argues. The case-load
in the Domestic Court virtually doubled from the 1920s to
the 1930s as probation officers and social workers compiled
bulging files on every family member, whether or not any of
them had been in conflict with the law.

One reason why only a handful of towns outside Toronto
established family courts in this period was the cost, but
another more important reason was the wariness of the
higher courts about the constitutional legality of domestic
courts' declared jurisdiction. In this respect, we can see how

the formal law, with its traditional attention to matters of procedure and constitutionality, provided a break against highly interventionist forms of moral regulation. As one Hamilton magistrate, who administered the Juvenile Delinquents Act, privately admitted: 'we shut our eyes to legal technicalities and rules of evidence in the interest of domestic peace.' Appellate courts tend to be fussy about 'technicalities' when it came to defining jurisdictional boundaries. In 1937, in ruling on two different cases that questioned the jurisdiction of juvenile or family courts to order support payments, the Alberta and Ontario Courts of Appeal declared these powers beyond the lower courts' jurisdictions. The involvement of so many extra-legal actors – social workers, psychiatrists, Big Brothers or Sisters – in the surveillance of citizens and the enforcement of court orders troubled the legal hierarchy. But only one year later, the federal Supreme Court made a landmark ruling which affirmed the Domestic Court's right to preside over a broad range of family disputes. More significantly, the ruling recognized that the family court's legal short-cuts and improvisations were justified, given the court's 'special character.'

Provincial mothers' allowance programes also combated forces believed to lead to family breakdown. The obvious difference was that mothers applied for assistance directly from the state rather than from husbands. Between 1916 and 1920, five provinces established mothers' allowance schemes, with Quebec joining the group in 1937, and New Brunswick and Prince Edward Island in the 1940s. Designed to aid 'those mothers who, through no fault of their own, found themselves unable to support their children,' such schemes, advocates hoped, would allow deserving subjects the means to raise their children to be 'useful citizens.' But instituting mothers' pensions provided new mechanisms for moral regulation. Margaret Little argues that assistance in this period was a matter of discretion, rather than a right. Applicants had to demonstrate proof both of poverty and of 'good moral character' in order to be qualify. Under the

Indian Act, status Indian women could not apply for assistance, and most provinces also excluded unmarried or divorced women. Any evidence of wrongdoing – drinking, visiting dancehalls, or socializing with men – disqualified applicants, as did tips from neighbours that they had bumped into reportedly deceased husbands.

Mothers' allowances were not universally applauded by social welfare spokespersons, however. Fearing that pension schemes would encourage 'the unfit' to breed, Charlotte Whitton was an active opponent of the schemes which, in her mind, sapped 'self-dependence ... the very basis of initiative, enterprise, and strength of character.' In spite of the rigorous moral and economic screening which already reduced the flood of needy applicants to a trickle, Whitton complained that 'careful supervision' ought to go hand in hand with hand-outs. Again, as we saw with the assistance courts provided in collecting support payments, state aid was predicated on moral surveillance. Unlike the post–Second World War era, which introduced rights-based welfare to Canada, the interwar period was characterized by a hybrid form of welfare-cum-charity, in which those who received aid had to adhere to moral norms in order to merit help. New forms of surveillance and assistance were justified as a means to save families, but they simultaneously fulfilled the greater project to build up character and ideal citizenship.

The Coming Generation

Similar ambivalence was felt over the touchy subject of birth control. Since the early twentieth century, eugenically-minded doctors such as Helen MacMurchy and C.K. Clarke had campaigned tirelessly for the isolation of the 'feeble-minded.' Carrie Derek, a Montreal feminist and a professor of botany, went so far as to advocate medically ordered sterilization. For her, the metaphor of weeding out the 'unfit' came easily. Experts were not so enthusiastic when it came to supporting individual access to safe and effective birth control, however. Emily Murphy, Edmonton Police Court Magistrate, was as concerned as anyone about the believed breeding propensities of deviants and criminals, but she was dead set against birth control. In a 1928 *Chatelaine* article on companionate marriage, she warned that birth control could be lethal, and that it would only encourage a form of marriage little more than 'an agreement between a flirt and a philanderer.' Pope Pius XI, an even greater authority (at least to Catholics), clarified the Catholic Church's traditional opposition to birth control in a 1930 Bull which also took aim at related threats to family life – divorce and companionate (as opposed to child-focused) marriage. Thus, those who argued for sterilization or birth control to prune back the unfit risked censure in conservative quarters until the Depression.

Although a few maverick doctors and academics openly supported birth control (especially for the poor), the fledgling movement was panned in the 1920s as a fringe cause. The 1927 conviction and five-year penitentiary sentence of the Ontario Birth Control League's leader, the aged Dr O.C.J. Withrow, was a major victory for anti–birth control forces, since the victim of his clumsy abortion operation had been a wealthy Anglo-Celtic woman – precisely the sort of woman whom the state counted on to raise 'fit' Canadians. Had it not been for the Depression and state fears about the communists' political threat and the economic drain of the unemployed, historians Angus McLaren and Arlene Tigar McLaren argue, the birth-control movement might have drifted for decades.

Out of desperation, individual women, often assisted by their husbands, boyfriends, co-workers, or family members, knowingly violated the law to control their fertility. Illegally obtained instrument- and drug-induced abortions could indeed be lethal, as coroners' reports frequently revealed. But safer, relatively reliable forms of birth control, such as condoms and diaphragms, were possible to acquire. A discreet conversation with a neighbour, a nod to a pharmacist, or a desperate plea to a trusted family doctor might net a man or a woman contraceptive advice and devices, but open discussion, let alone purchase, of birth control was out of the question. This was the case until the late 1920s, when eugenically-minded businessman A.R. Kaufman began to challenge legal prohibitions openly.

In 1933 Kaufman established the Parents' Information Bureau, whose purpose was to distribute contraceptive information and kits to interested parties. Women in Depression-era Canada were evidently eager to learn: his offices had distributed more than 120,000 packages by 1942. A decade after Withrow was sent to prison, Kaufman, too, faced a legal challenge when one of his clinic workers, Dorothea Palmer, was charged with violating section 179 of the Criminal Code. In the midst of the Depression, everything had changed, however. Palmer was acquitted, and the birth-control movement was given a tacit seal of approval.

Kaufman's bureau continued its work unmolested, largely because powerful conservatives, including Emily Murphy, came to see birth control as a convenient cure for the Depression. Kaufman boldly predicted that widely distributed birth control would reduce the ranks of the poor and the weak. As he stated in 1937, providing cheap contraceptives to the unemployed would reduce the 'unintelligent and penniless who unfortunately constitute an increasing percentage of the total population.' In the darkest days of the Depression, the federal government succumbed to the cold fiscal logic of winking at birth control (even if it took another thirty-two years for the government to declare publicly that the 'state has no business in the bedrooms of the nation').

In Quebec, the Catholic Church remained a more important source of family regulation. The powerful voice of the Catholic Church, and the reluctance of the provincial government to support heretical birth-controllers, left the province with the nation's highest birth rate (until the

1950s). But conservative clergy were also instrumental in ensuring that forced sterilization laws, which were introduced in Alberta and British Columbia, were never imposed on Quebeckers.

The ABCs of Citizenship

Family aid was deemed suitable only if it could inculcate values and enforce behavioural norms. But what sorts of norms were to prevail? Canadians differed, sometimes violently, when they tried to determine how their children ought to be taught. In the postwar period, those who favoured state-controlled compulsory education, geared towards the promotion of pro-British Protestant values, won those struggles in every province but Quebec. In the first decades of the twentieth century, earlier victories for Catholic education or instruction in languages other than English were whittled away to nil. To preserve democracy and British values against the threat of 'foreign' ideologies, particularly communism, all children had to learn how to be 'proper' Canadians. As one educator insisted, compulsory state education was vital to nation-building: 'The development of a united and intelligent Canadian citizenship actuated by the highest British ideals of justice, tolerance, and fair play should be accepted without question as a fundamental aim of the provincial school system.' The institutional power of the Catholic Church in Quebec was sufficient to resist this national movement, but religious and racial minorities who, for their own reasons, rejected the right of the state to regulate education were less successful.

Education for citizenship training was first imposed on status Indians, as Brian Titley and others have argued. Native leaders were often ambivalent about education that offered children a slim possibility of economic advancement, yet was based on alien languages, faith, and culture, completely out of step with traditional forms of learning. 'We are Indians, and we intend to remain Indians,' one chief argued: 'I don't want schools because I want the children to be happy and free from restraint.' Industrial and boarding-schools had failed miserably, and had left aboriginal children anything but happy. According to J.R. Miller, pupils regularly escaped; parents refused to respect the school calendar; children suffered from inadequate heating, ventilation, and diets; and tuberculosis raged in many institutions. Although the federal government phased out industrial schools, it instituted a new residential school system in 1923, and appointed truancy officers, who, by 1930, were empowered to impose penalties to compel all Indian children between the ages of seven and sixteen to attend. Dismissing the coerciveness and insensitivity of the scheme, the Indian Affairs department determined that residential schools met a great need: 'there is a growing conviction on the part of our wards that their children must be better fitted for the future ... they are turning towards education to prepare themselves for encroaching civilization.'

Compulsory schooling of children also offered an indirect route to regulating non-Native parents and families. Non–English-speaking immigrants were objects of assimilation, but the group which suffered the most coercive attempts to impose state education in the interwar period were the Doukhobors, a radical Christian sect which rejected all forms of state intervention in civil life, from the registration of births and marriages to compulsory military service. John McLaren notes that Doukhobors, like professional educators, believed that children should be taught how best to regulate themselves: 'To us, education means being a good Doukhobor. That is, to love all living things and to do no evil, not to shoot, not to eat meat, not to smoke, not to drink liquor. We teach these things to our children.' The only problem was that they (like the chief who did not want schools, Christianity, or the law on his reserve) thought that traditional communities, not the state, knew best how to carry out this mission.

In Saskatchewan and British Columbia, home to many of Canada's Doukobors by the 1920s, provincial education authorities did not take Doukhobor parents' refusal to send their children to public schools lightly. Parents were frequently fined, and even jailed. British Columbia's provincial Public Schools Act was rarely invoked against parents who were simply too needy or neglectful to send their children to school, but police used it to seize entire Doukhobor communities' goods, and Doukhobor parents were fined as much as $50 for violating school-attendance laws.

In the face of persistent non-compliance, and even school burnings, the federal government added a new offence, 'parading in the nude' (a traditional expression of Doukhobor defiance against the state), to the Criminal Code in 1931. The following year, some 600 Doukhobors in British Columbia were arrested under this new regulation after they assembled unclothed to protest compulsory-schooling laws. Close to 400 of their children instantly became wards of the state. They were summarily institutionalized in industrial schools, orphanages, and Anglo-Celtic foster homes, where, it was naïvely hoped, they would disavow their unconventional beliefs. During the Depression, however, the costs of Draconian moral regulation could not justify the goal of forced assimilation. By the 1933, most of the children were quietly released to Doukhobors who promised to send them to school.

Using public education to strip away undesirable cultural traits of religious minorities and Native people was hardly subtle. But in the postwar period, educating all children came to be seen as a critical building-block for the nation. Suspicious of this secular philosophy, the Catholic Church in Quebec remained resolutely anti-statist, with no apparent ill-effects to children, according to Ruby Heap. In fact, literacy rates and school-attendance figures were actually higher in Quebec than they were where official truancy officers patrolled for slackers. English-speaking Protestants were more inclined to see properly regulated state schooling as a boon. For them, the coercive elements of public education were scarcely visible since state schooling promoted mainstream Christian and pro-British values. Far less drastic an approach to social betterment than eugenics, compulsory education (as minority children and their parents knew well) none the less complemented more overtly coercive forms of moral regulation.

Canadianization for the Nation

Seeking out immigrants who would become 'moral and patriotic' citizens, like educating youth for the responsibilities of civic life, began to attract greater state attention. As the number of immigrants to Canada declined in the interwar period, more rigorous screening procedures were put into place. Barbara Roberts and Donald Avery have argued that the federal government attempted to attract the most desirable immigrants – not surprisingly, British, white, English-speaking, and Protestant. Others might be admitted to meet demands of mining and logging interests (not to mention ladies on the look-out for maids). But no matter how economically desirable an immigrant might be, officials in the Department of Immigration were prepared to reject the 'unfit,' the politically dangerous, and the racially 'inferior.' In this sense, the discretionary powers of immigration officers complemented pro-family regulations, eugenics, and compulsory-education schemes in the interwar period. Determining who could become or remain Canadian was one more way to shape the moral character of the nation.

Immigrants, like Indians, were scrutinized more thoroughly than others for signs of disloyalty to, or deviance from, idealized Canadian virtues. In fact, the investigation of cultural rites practised by Natives (whom the state could *not* deport) set precedents for the surveillance of immigrants whom the state *could* deport. Although revisions to the Indian Act in 1918 produced a sudden rise in prosecutions for potlatching (135 individuals were charged between 1918 and 1922), its symbolic import remained the same: to be a 'good Indian' required individuals to abandon non-Christian, 'uncivilized' ways, and to adopt Canadian values. Becoming a good Canadian citizen implied similar commitments; the difference was that immigrants who failed to measure up could find themselves subjected to distinct forms of regulation.

In the interwar period, several immigration-related acts swung the doors open wide for some, while jamming it shut on others. Although evidence of Britons' lax morals and left-wing political ideologies mounted over the 1920s, immigration-policy makers assumed that white, English-speaking, Protestant immigrants would uphold democracy, practise Christianity, and embrace economic individualism. In 1922, Canada worked with England to implement the Empire Settlement Act, which funded and monitored colonization schemes for emigrating Britons. For instance, between 1923 and 1931, almost 24,000 British women came to Canada under this scheme as household workers. Whenever economic downturns generated pressure to restrict the number of immigrants (as it did in the early 1920s, and in the Depression), the intake of British immigrants, and others, declined. Nevertheless, Britons were consistently subjected to the fewest restrictions imposed on immigrants to Canada.

Quantity did not guarantee quality, however. Many British immigrants were female domestics, recruited by employers disheartened by native-born Canadian women's preference for factory, office, and retail work. Complaints about British domestics' loose morals and lack of appropriate skills, combined with doubts about British menfolk (some of whom had been ringleaders of the Winnipeg General Strike), led to demands for improved screening procedures. As psychiatrist C.K. Clarke claimed, 'the ideals which have counted for so much in the past in keeping this young country sane, and an example of virility, are in danger as a result of the type of immigration that has been fostered of late years.' Organizations such as the United Farm Women of Alberta, along with Charlotte Whitton's Child and Family Welfare Council, pressed for restrictions to protect Canada from 'feeble-minded, epileptic, tubercular, dumb, blind, illiterate, criminal, and anarchistic' immigrants.

Although such drastic immigration restrictions were never formally enacted, the federal government filtered the undesirable through administrative procedures. Those judged to be 'unfit' could be deported with little opportunity to appeal. For men, unemployment or affiliation in left-wing organizations accounted for the bulk of deportations; for women, evidence (however thin) of immorality was most likely to lead to a deportation order. According to Barbara Roberts, surveillance of immigrant women was enhanced after 1919, when the Women's Division of the Department of Immigration was established. Women officers in the division monitored all female immigrants for signs of maladjustment or evidence of misrepresentation. Single women were deported if investigators discovered they were actually married; so were women who had children out of wedlock, women who appeared to court more than one man, women who carried venereal disease, and women who had tuberculosis. When the Women's Division tabulated the reasons why almost 700 women, recruited under the Empire Settlement Aftercare program, had been deported, they found that more than 500 had been apprehended for 'being a public charge.' But this offence was merely a catch-all description for a host of ill-defined moral failings, including illegitimacy, 'immorality,' 'bad conduct,' 'mental deficiency,' 'vagrancy,' and unemployment. During the Depression, married women were sometimes deported if their *husbands* were unemployed, a practice which, like family-court maintenance orders, reinforced the homemaker breadwinner marital norm.

Non-British and non-white immigrants faced more overt

forms of immigration restrictions, irrespective of their physical, moral, or mental fitness. Race alone was reason enough to disqualify blacks and Chinese who wished to attain Canadian citizenship. Although Canada, unlike Australia, did not introduce a formal 'whites only' policy, the Department of Immigration singled out these two groups as undesirables who could never be assimilated on account of their supposedly indelible racial inferiority. Since 1910, section 38, subsection 'c,' of the Immigration Act had permitted immigration agents to prohibit potential immigrants who were members of races considered 'unsuitable for the climate' of Canada. The act did not mention blacks, but that was hardly necessary for racist restrictions to take place, as the exclusion of black Oklahoman immigrants to the Prairies in the 1910s had confirmed. In contrast, the Chinese were subjected to a revenue-generating form of screening, in the guise of an immigrant head tax. Under mounting pressure from anti-Asiatic leagues, farmers' organizations, retail merchants, trade unions, and British Columbia politicians, the federal government resolved to stem Chinese immigration altogether. The Chinese Immigration Act of 1923 was ironically named, for it excluded virtually anyone of Chinese descent from immigrating to Canada.

While European immigrants were more likely to be feared as potential anarchists or Bolsheviks, blacks and Chinese were persistently portrayed as moral threats. By the 1920s, the drug 'menace' had become a powerful new signifier of postwar moral disorder – the source of which, campaigners claimed, was foreigners. Complaints about sabbath-breakers, gamblers, and white slavers had already mobilized racist stereotypes, but the lobbying efforts to strengthen drug laws revived fears of racial mongrelization and moral corruption. When the mass circulation *MacLean's Magazine* published a series of articles by Edmonton police magistrate Emily Murphy on the evils of drugs, readers' fears reached a fever pitch, and Parliament responded accordingly. Between 1919 and 1921 it passed amendments to the Opium Act which imposed heavier sentences (such as seven-year maximums for trafficking), while augmenting police search powers. In 1922 (after Murphy's articles were published in book form as *The Black Candle*) a further amendment allowed judges the option to deport aliens convicted of drug offences, no matter how minor.

Fears of racial degeneration were lodged at the heart of debates over the drug menace. For instance, *The Black Candle* included provocative pictures of dissipated white women, lounging in bed with black men. These images help explain why cannabis (a drug Canadian authorities associated with U.S. Southerners) suddenly ended up on revised lists of prohibited drugs. With no firmer evidence than Mackenzie King had offered, Murphy convinced the Department of Health that people who smoked marijuana became 'raving maniacs ... liable to kill or indulge in any form of violence to other persons, using the most savage methods of cruelty.' Pictures of dingy opium dens, peopled by wizened Chinese addicts, were no less shocking to white readers. So strong was the association between drugs and foreignness that the 1923 amended Opium and Narcotic Act stipulated that every alien convicted was now to be deported automatically.

Provincial and municipal governments did not have the power to exclude or deport 'undesirables,' yet they shared the same concern that Chinese people *not* be permitted to form families in Canada, particularly if marital unions involved Chinese men and white women. Saskatchewan, British Columbia, Manitoba, and Ontario prohibited the employment of white women by Asian employers. Municipal by-laws and licensing restrictions permitted flexible, and subtler, means for local governments to restrict Chinese men's access to white women employees. Saskatchewan's Act to Prevent the Employment of Female Labour in Certain Capacities was typical: 'No person shall employ in any capacity any white woman or girl ... to reside or lodge in or to work in ... any restaurant, laundry, or other place of business or amusement owned, kept or managed by any Japanese, Chinaman, or other Oriental person.' Passed in 1912, it was tested in 1924 when Regina restaurateur Yee Clun contested city council's refusal to grant him a licence to employ white women. Although Yee successfully appealed the decision in the provincial court, Constance Backhouse shows that his victory prompted legislators to drop 'Chinese employers' from the text of the act, while allowing municipalities to refuse or revoke licences 'at their discretion.' Like informal restrictions against blacks on the basis of their 'unsuitability' for the climate, 'protective' labour legislation provided flexible legal means to regulate Canada's racial mix and, by extension, its moral character.

Although anti-Chinese protective legislation represented a victory for middle-class female women who feared that Chinese men were sexual predators, most white women who actually worked for Chinese employers did not appreciate being 'protected' out of their jobs. When Toronto waitresses heard that Ontario's restrictive legislation was about to be enforced in 1928, eighty of them sent a petition to the lieutenant-governor, stressing that they feared for their livelihood. Besides, they argued, their bosses were perfect gentlemen: 'your Petitioners are well satisfied with their present employment and have no complaints whatever to make as regards their employers. WHEREFORE your Petitioners humbly pray that [we] may be able to retain [our] present means of livelihood.' The Ontario act, like those in many other provinces, appears to have been enforced spottily, but the acts themselves were overt reminders that regulating race and gender was critical to the maintenance of moral order.

Conclusion

The struggle to keep Canada 'clean' began with campaigns to encourage marriage and the formation of 'fit' families, and it branched out to the larger goal of establishing a nation of citizens who could fulfil high expectations for Canada's place in the postwar world. The Depression dashed hopes for prosperity, but it also seriously challenged the ideal of the stable, heterosexual family headed by a breadwinning father and homemaking mother. But state intervention into family life did not begin or end with campaigns to keep the Depression-era family afloat. Rather, the roots of regulation through social-welfare legislation reach down to the late 1910s and early 1920s, when compulsory education, minimum-wage acts, and mothers' allowance legislation was implemented in most parts of the country. Through juvenile, women's, and domestic courts the state intervened as never before to enforce normative visions of gender roles within the family. At the same time, segregation and sterilization of the 'unfit,' along with relaxed restrictions against birth control information and devices, showed that the state (outside of Quebec) was prepared to interfere with 'nature' when moral fitness of the nation was at stake. Various strategies were also introduced to determine which races would be stirred into the Canadian mélange. Segregation and coercive tutelage were the solutions for Native peoples; white resistance and administrative discretion kept out most blacks (save those recruited to be miners and maids); and the Chinese were legally barred, both from entering Canada and from working freely if already resident. As Dr C.K. Clarke had made clear in the aftermath of the Winnipeg General Strike, building a great nation depended on the proper mix of racially, physically, morally, and politically fit citizens.

6

The Moral Crises of Capital

The 'return to normalcy' after the Great War involved a return to a traditional gender and sexual order, but also a return to a rigidly defined political and ideological order. The government increasingly regulated marriage, the family, immigration, and drugs and alcohol, but it also stifled political dissent in the name of protecting the 'Canadian way of life.' During the war, the federal government had interned thousands of Austrians and Germans, as well as southern and eastern European men – enemy aliens whose loyalty was suspect because of both their nationality and, in some cases, their earlier involvement with revolutionary workers' organizations, like the Industrial Workers of the World. After the armistice, many Anglo-Canadians remained suspicious of these 'dangerous foreigners,' believing now that they might follow the example of the newly ascendant Communist government in Russia.

Their worst suspicions seemed confirmed on 15 May, 1919, when a dispute between the Winnipeg Building Trades workers and the city's Building Trades Council escalated into a general strike. Nearly 30,000 women and men, many of them non-unionized, walked off the job in support of the strikers' demands for higher wages, better conditions, and union recognition. In short order, the city was divided. On one side were the strikers, who, if the anti-strike press were to be believed, were 'aliens,' little more than bomb-throwing Bolsheviks who would stop at nothing to bring revolution to the Red River. On the other stood the self-named 'citizens,' an alliance of business and professional people committed to turning back the red tide, and protecting the 'Canadian way of life.'

To meet the crisis, the federal government amended the Criminal Code and Immigration Act in 1919 to stifle dissent and to lay the legal groundwork for deporting those who dared persist. Though the general strike was crushed, these 'emergency' measures, passed ostensibly 'for the duration,' remained in force throughout the 1930s. In addition, 1919 afforded the government an opportunity to reorganize its federal police force. The Mounties, born after the Red River Rebellion, were expanded in the wake of another, this time to fight a different set of 'red men.' Throughout the Dirty Thirties, the Mounties spied on, harassed, and helped to deport Canada's Communists.

This war against the reds was waged simultaneously with a war against the unemployed, using similar weaponry. The Great Depression put thousands of people out of work and created a moral crisis for all levels of government: how could they give relief without corrupting its recipients? In part, they tried to avoid the problem in the first place by deporting unemployed immigrants for becoming 'public charges.' Those they could not deport, they subjected to a system of relief, which, while aimed at improving their material condition, also disciplined them by imposing particular values regarding poverty, gender, and ethnicity.

This chapter looks at deportation and relief as legal and quasi-legal forms of moral regulation. It explores why the Communists and the unemployed were construed as threats, and how, in targeting them, the government actually regulated many others, reproducing in the process social norms about gender, ethnicity, and marital status. But as with the state's other efforts at regulation, the results were partial, uneven, and contradictory.

The 'Iron Heel of Ruthlessness'

The linkages between radicalism and 'foreign elements' in the postwar labour revolt led some people to the conclusion that a revised immigration policy was just the sort of ideological prophylactic Canada needed. Donald Avery points out that, after 1919, the federal government moved to make ideological conformability and assimilability, rather than economic considerations, the primary determinants of the country's immigration policy. Organized labour, the Great War Veterans' Association, and a variety of nativist organizations lobbied the federal government for more restrictions. Even the Canadian Manufacturers' Association, a group that had backed almost unrestricted immigration in the name of economic progress (and cheap labour), lent its support to the changes to block the immigration of 'those whose political and social beliefs unfit them for assimilation with Canadians.' These efforts, along with rising unemployment in the early 1920s, led the federal government in 1922 to make British citizens and Americans preferred immigrants, despite the prominent role which British-born radicals had played in the general strikes of 1919, and despite the historical association in Canadians' minds of the United States with immorality. In 1923, the most openly racist immigration law was passed: the Chinese Immigration Act.

Not all Canadians were happy with these changes, especially those eager to exploit workers who would put up with low wages. The Railway Association of Canada insisted that their members be allowed to import southern and eastern European men to meet a labour shortage in railway construction, attributable in part to an alleged 'aversion of the native-born and other Canadians for this class of work.' Owners of construction and resource industries had similar concerns. Without continued economic growth, the question of the character of Canadian life would be a moot point. These were powerful arguments, all the more so because the best wishes of the Department of Immigration to fashion a white Canada had actually encouraged few British or American emigrants to come. Confronted with this situation, the federal government abandoned its restrictive policy. In 1923 it eliminated the ban on emigrants from Germany and its wartime allies, and in 1925 it passed the Railway Agreement, which put all European immigrants, regardless of their country of origin, on the same footing as those from the United States and Great Britain. As we saw in chapter 5, the economic costs attached to regulation could sometimes force governments to compromise their moral agenda.

As for organized labour, economic self-interest blended with moral, and particularly ethnocentric concerns about threats to a uniformly Anglo-Saxon Canada. In 1928 the Trades and Labour Congress recommended that no fewer than 75 per cent of all Canadian immigrants be English-speaking. Ultimately there was a broad-based coalition against the Railway Agreement, which, on the left, included representatives of labour, and, on the right, people like Conservative party leader R.B. Bennett, who worried that unrestricted immigration would weaken the Anglo-Saxon character of Canada, and the Canadian Chiefs of Police, who wanted to fingerprint all immigrants. As remnants of the community-based regulators who had exercised great influence in pre-Confederation Canada, the Ku Klux Klan, then at the height of its influence, added its condemnation of the 'slag and scum that refuse to assimilate.' In the face of this mounting pressure and a rapidly deteriorating economy, the federal government revoked the Railway Agreement in 1928.

As it turned out, the Anglo-Saxon citizenry need not have worried. Even while the Railway Agreement was in force – and long after it had been revoked – the federal government had been busy 'shovelling out' those immigrants it deemed unfit or undesirable. Under section 40 of the Immigration Act, immigrants who had been in Canada for less than five years (those 'without domicile') and who were found guilty of 'moral turpitude,' or a criminal offence, or who became public charges, or who otherwise breached the act (for example, entering Canada under false pretences), could be deported. In the midst of the Winnipeg General Strike, the federal government added a new provision to the Immigration Act. Under section 41 *anyone* who was not born in Canada could be deported for advocating 'the overthrow by force or violence ... constituted law and authority.' This included not only recent arrivals, but also those who had established 'domicile' (that is, had been there for at least five years), and those who had been naturalized.

Political offences stand out as the only ones for which people with domicile could, without legal protection, be deported. The Mounties began vetting prospective immigrants and naturalized citizens. In 1926, the force was fingerprinting prospective immigrants and checking their prints against those in their criminal files. Nine years later, it was printing 2,200 naturalized citizens a month. Information on 'undesirables' was shared with the American and British authorities, and set the machinery to deport them into motion. A purely administrative process, deportation occurred behind closed doors, unchecked by any public scrutiny, and conducted according to Department of Immigration rules, rather than any formal legally sanctioned procedures.

Many of the deportees were immigrants who resisted the efforts launched by the schools, churches, and other institutions to Canadianize them. But the best-known deportees in the interwar period also held a set of political beliefs that in the eyes of the Canadian government disqualified them from citizenship: they were 'agitators' and 'radicals' – usually Communists or Communist sympathizers, very loosely (if at all) defined.

Long before the Communist Party of Canada was formed in 1921, the Canadian state had been actively engaged in the surveillance and deportation of suspected radicals. The legal foundation for doing more than simply trailing 'subversives,' such as members of the Industrial Workers of the World, was laid in 1918 and 1919, when the federal government banned organizations whose purpose was to bring about 'any governmental, industrial, or economic change in Canada by use of force, violence, or physical injury to person or property,' or which advocated or defended such a course of action. Belonging to or supporting such an organization in any way – even wearing any of its badges or insignia or possessing its literature – was defined as 'seditious' under section 98 of the Criminal Code. More significantly, it was punishable by imprisonment for up to twenty years and deportation for those not born in Canada. Section 98 made *beliefs* rather than actions the basis of criminal prosecution. Simple membership amounted to a crime. Like the laws establishing other status offences such as prostitution, section 98 placed the onus on the accused person to prove he or she was not guilty – in this case, not a member of a 'seditious' organization. This 'reverse onus' requirement was a feature of all 'morals' offences, and suggests the wider connections the government made between politics and morality. Anarchism and Bolshevism threatened to corrupt the morality of the dominion itself.

The events of 1919 weakened the link between ethnicity and disloyalty. While 'dangerous foreigners' might still be the agents of a Communist revolution, the real threat to Canadian security was considered to be rooted in Communist ideology, not ethnicity. Ideology was much harder to detect, however, as Larry Hannant notes. To do so, the federal government began to reorganize its security forces in early 1919, just in time for the General Strike. On the eve of that reorganization, four different agencies reported on security matters. The main one, the Royal North-West Mounted Police, consisted of just 303 officers, the same size as it was at its founding in 1873, when its primary task was fighting other 'red men' on the prairies. By September

1919, the new Royal Canadian Mounted Police (RCMP) were 1,600 strong, having expanded the number of detectives and secret agents to fight communism. The RCMP infiltrated labour organizations and began to keep systematic records of subversive organizations and individuals. The force combined fighting crime and buttressing a liberal-democratic political order in its Criminal Investigation Branch, which housed fingerprinting, criminal investigations, and political intelligence under the same roof, the first two functions cloaking the last, which was not even given statutory authority until much later, in 1934.

For an organization founded in a Guelph barn and numbering, at its height in the 1930s, only 16,000 card-carrying members, the Communist Party of Canada certainly created a sensation. To many, the party and its sympathizers posed a moral threat. Their program of revolution and the abolition of private property was antithetical to the capitalist and bourgeois values of the Canadian mainstream. That threat often seemed even more encompassing. In the popular press, the 'Bolshevik' was always a hairy, dirty, 'foreign-looking' man, thus comprising a danger that was racial and sexual as well as ideological. The Communist Party's pronouncements on the 'woman question' rejected the notion of separate spheres and the connection between women and domesticity and morality. The private sphere was as political as the public, Communists stated, and was the source of women's oppression. Capitalism was built on relegating women to 'household drudgery,' but in a Communist society, relations between the sexes would be more equal; women would be recognized as workers, and not simply as mothers. Some Communists, particularly the Finns, rejected marriage outright, attacking what mainstream Canadians considered the bedrock of national morality. The party made a point of comparing the greater emancipation of Russian women who had access to a liberalized divorce law, birth control, and abortion. Predictably, in Quebec, the campaign against the 'red menace' was led by the Roman Catholic Church.

The party's successful organizing efforts in the late 1920s and 1930s gave suspected moral danger concrete form. The Workers' Unity League, Farmers' Unity League, Canadian Labour Defence League, and National Association of Unemployed Workers supplemented the Communist Party with a loose and unaffiliated membership of more than 50,000. Labour candidates (some of them actually Communists) got elected to municipal councils and some provincial legislatures. In response, Prime Minister R.B. Bennett promised to crush communism with an 'iron heel of ruthlessness.' In 1931, the federal government amended the Criminal Code to make the Communist Party an illegal association by virtue of its policies, not its actions. Hoping to buttress its support, especially in Quebec, Bennett's Conservatives were keen play the morality card by taking a tough line on communism using the newly strengthened section 98. After months of surveillance, the RCMP had fingered eighty-two 'reds' across Canada for deportation and, in August 1931, moved in to make its first high-profile arrests. Tim Buck, Tom McEwen, and Malcolm Bruce, good Anglo-Saxons all, were collared, as were five other men who actually fit the common stereotype of the Canadian Bolshevik: Sam Carr represented the Communist Party's left-wing Jewish component; Amos Hill, the Finnish connection; Tomo Cacic, the Croatian; and John Boychuk and Matthew Popovic, the Ukrainian element. The 'Toronto Eight,' as they were called, were convicted of seditious conspiracy, put through what amounted to a show trial, sentenced to between three and five years, and (with one exception) slated for deportation after serving their sentences in Kingston Penitentiary.

Though the government was forced to release the Eight in 1934 in light of increasing public sympathy, the harassment of Canada's Communists continued. Lesser-known party activists and rank-and-file members did not enjoy public support and media coverage, and thus were more easily deported – and for lesser 'crimes' too. Whereas Tim Buck had been arrested because he was head of the party, and Malcolm Bruce because he was editor of the *Worker*, scores of obscure workers were shipped out for any number of seemingly minor activities: marching in a parade against the government; taking part in a relief strike; possessing Communist literature; or simply being a vagrant. Even those who protested this Draconian policy towards subversives became morally suspect. As the editor of Toronto's *Mail and Empire* noted, making the connection between dissent and citizenship, 'the majority of those who have a gripe about police interference ... are not Canadian by birth or persons who have lived all their lives under British institutions. They need reminding that the laws of Canada are binding upon them. No sovietism or other form of anarchism they have been indoctrinated in [through] alien countries or by alien teaching will find a footing here.' Given the broad definition of subversive behaviour and the scope and intensity of surveillance, the RCMP and the Department of Immigration were really engaged in what amounted to a war against the working class and their 'sympathizers.' Though Communism and Communists were the formal targets of regulation, the net cast by the government was much wider, snaring a variety of dissaffected Canadians.

Significantly, Canada's growing right-wing organizations did not find themselves entangled in the same regulatory net. Groups like the KKK had a membership of 40,000 in Saskatchewan alone in the late 1920s and early 1930s, and fascist organizations like Ontario's Swastika Clubs and Adrien Arcand's Parti National Social Chrétien (National Social Christian Party) also found significant support. All of these organizations criticized the status quo and advocated violent change, but because they targeted those on the margins – immigrants and Jews – and not the Canadian political structure *per se*, they were not considered moral threats. Though watched, they were not prosecuted or deported for their actions. Indeed, as part of their strategy to increase their support in Quebec in the lead up to the 1935 federal election, Bennett's Conservatives hired Arcand as the party's provincial publicity director, hoping to cash in on the fascist's charisma.

Other levels of government provided covering fire in an attempt to knock out 'Bolshevik' communications. Using tactics that had been deployed against the Wobblies in the first decade of the twentieth century, the Toronto municipal council passed a by-law prohibiting street-corner political speeches, while others limited free speech to those who could speak English – a clear indication of the continuing linkages they made between radicalism and foreigners. In Vancouver and Toronto, city councillors threatened to rescind the theatre licences of the Workers' Experimental Theatre, a workers' group whose plays were considered inflammatory.

Perhaps the best example of the campaign against communism comes from Maurice Duplessis's Quebec, where church and state were allied against the reds, and where the Communist Party was hampered by its own insensitivity to cultural differences. Unlike the Communists, Duplessis's agitators and local priests spoke in a language that working-class Quebeckers (who might otherwise have been sympathetic to the Communist cause) could understand. To protect its citizenry further, the Quebec government passed the Act respecting Communistic Propaganda, more commonly known as the Padlock Law, in 1937. The repeal of section 98 just a year before had left the Quebec élite, and particularly the virulently anti-Communist Catholic Church, nonplussed. The new provincial law empowered the attorney general to close any building used for propagating 'communism or bolshevism,' and to destroy any printed material that professed these ideas. Neither Communism nor Bolshevism was defined. There was no need to, for as Premier Duplessis himself asserted, 'Communism can be felt.' 'Subversive' magazines like the *Canadian Forum* and *Labour World* were seized. *Time*, an American publication not known for its left-leaning tendencies, observed (quoting a suppressed Quebec journal) that the province 'was a paradise for capitalists and a hell for workers.'

The campaign against communism was an integral part of nation-building, concerned as it was with maintaining a particular set of political values by eliminating those who professed different ones. Those who dared to expose the excesses of capitalism or to propose alternatives, as the Communists did, had to be made to comply forcibly, at gunpoint if necessary, but preferably through surveillance, deportation, and censorship. Both the Immigration Act and the Criminal Code were used to secure a social and political order that was capitalist and not socialist or communist, Anglo-Saxon and not 'ethnic,' and one that protected the propertied and married, as opposed to the single and propertyless.

Down 'n' Out – And Deported

Sending 'dangerous foreigners' home did not entirely remove the moral danger facing the 'Canadian way of life.' Canadians did not have to read *Das Kapital* or *The Communist Manifesto* to question the justice of the status quo. In the late 1920s and 1930s, the breadlines and soup kitchens, the 'jungles' – encampments of homeless on the outskirts of cities – the relief marches, and the men riding the rails were enough to suggest that something was deeply wrong. As Amos Hill, one of the Toronto Eight, observed during his 1931 trial, 'it is not necessary for us [the Communist Party] to spread discontent among the Canadian people. It is being done without our assistance.'

During the Dirty Thirties, unemployment, for all intents and purposes, became a status offence, just like prostitution and communism, and it precipitated a range of regulatory responses, from deportation and incarceration, to rehabilitation, all of which fell under the rubric of 'relief.' Like the war against communism, Canada's relief programs targeted one group (in this case, the poor), but the treatment they received varied according to region, ethnicity, gender, and marital status.

Deporting the unemployed was an important part of the federal government's 'relief' program and, as Shin Imai argues, an extension of the country's immigration policy. The practice of removing the poor had deep roots, going back to the seventeenth-century English law of settlement. According to that law, parishes were responsible for the welfare of all parishioners born within their boundaries (or 'settled' there). 'Strangers' who fell on hard times while living away from their home parishes could be sent back to their 'settlements,' where the costs of their upkeep would be born by those who had the primary responsibility. During the Great Depression of the 1930s, Canada began turning out the poor in a similar fashion and for similar reasons, but on a scale never before seen and over distances much greater than in nearby parishes. From 1930 to 1935, more than 17,000 men, women, and children were sent packing because, as the Department of Immigration put it, they had become 'public charges'; in other words, they were unemployed and on relief. Under section 40 of the Immigration Act, that meant they were liable to deportation.

As was the case with the war against communism, every level of government, and not just federal officials, joined in the struggle to regulate poverty. In fact, Canada's municipalities were the foot-soldiers in the unemployment war, echoing an earlier era of community regulation. Like the parishes of old, municipalities in the 1930s bore the brunt of the responsibility for relief, and, given the scale of unemployment, the possibility of deporting their problem had immense appeal. Federal and municipal officials differed on how to go about it, however. The federal government was much more cautious about illegalities, covering its tracks as much as possible, carefully crafting air-tight *post hoc* rationales for deporting the unemployed after their immigration officials had already signed warrants authorizing their deportation. Immigration officials constructed the unemployed as 'unemployable' – people who would not work or were not fit to work. Alternatively, they tried to show that the individuals in question had misrepresented themselves at the time they emigrated, or had a pre-existing condition (a disease or criminal record, for instance) that would have, if detected earlier, barred their entry. In essence, immigration officials tried to make the unemployed fit any of the categories listed under section 40 of the act, which specified conditions for deportation.

Municipal relief departments, on the other hand, faced mounting relief costs and little prospect of federal funding or an economic turn-around. Desperate city officials relied on more ham-fisted manoeuvres to mask their actions. In Winnipeg, for instance, the Relief department insisted that those applying for support sign a 'voluntary' deportation agreement. Other cities reported people who had received as little as $2 to $4 in relief as 'public charges' warranting deportation – a bald attempt to manipulate the federal immigration system to solve a municipal problem.

The whole scheme was exposed, however, when it became clear that the British-born were overrepresented among the unemployed. As they were sent home, an indignant hue and cry broke out. Deportation might be justified for 'foreigners' but to find Anglo-Celts among the flotsam and jetsam of the Great Depression was not only manifestly unfair but unsightly to civic leaders of British stock. Facing both international and domestic embarrassment, the federal government moved quickly to discipline municipalities and to modify federal immigration policy. The Immigration department would now use a formula to determine who among the unemployed would be deported. After 1930, even though the British made up the bulk of the unemployed, only 50 per cent of deportees were British-born. The government also took pains to construct British deportees as 'voluntary.' Canada was merely assisting in the 'repatriation' of unemployed Britons. Meanwhile, the department continued to threaten others, hoping to scare them into finding work or into leaving voluntarily.

Ironically, as the Depression worsened, it dawned on some unemployed people that deportation offered an opportunity to better their situation. At the least, it offered a ticket home, where families and community might provide support. Realizing that deportation might indeed be voluntary after all, the federal government did not want to turn into a 'booking agency' for homesick and out-of-work immigrants. Nor did they want the possibility of deportation to deter others from looking for work. The regulatory cure, it seemed, threatened to become as bad as the disease.

On the Dole

Just five weeks after his successful prime-ministerial campaign in 1930, R.B. Bennett's Conservatives passed what would be the first of three unemployment relief acts, earmarking an unprecedented $20 million for the down and out, ten times the amount spent in the previous decade for relief. Though during the election he had claimed that unemployment was a national problem calling for a national solution, his government handed over the $20 million grudgingly, and with a warning: relief, Bennett insisted, 'was primarily a provincial and municipal responsibility,' not a federal one; in any case, aid was offered only as a 'palliative' and not as a cure.

Though it was meant to alleviate hard times, the relief system simultaneously disciplined its recipients according to a particular set of values. At their core was a belief that poverty and unemployment were the result, in large measure of individual shortcomings. Political support for relief was always hesitant, since, as many relief administrators commented, relief encouraged people to think that one need not take responsibility for oneself or one's neighbours. In the language of the day, relief 'demoralized' its recipients, and, as one RCMP officer pointed out, it could also have unsettling political effects. 'I have seen men come into the office with tears in their eyes suffering humiliation at being forced to apply for assistance,' he reported. 'Today the very same men are demanding increases in relief and adopting an attitude that it is their inalienable right to receive relief ... As issued today ... it ... encourages them to develope [sic] socialistic ideas.'

As the Mountie's comment suggests, the concern about unemployment and the demoralizing effects of relief was really a concern about the effects unemployment and relief on Euro-Canadian *men*. The threat of women's politicization did not resonate with officials, nor has the image of women reduced to tears in relief offices earned a place in the mythology of the Great Depression. Relief programs reflected anxieties about masculinity as well as unemployment. They reflected the prevailing belief that work was the source of male dignity, and they were designed to preserve the gender norms at the root of social stability. The Conservatives therefore insisted that the bulk of federal money go towards public works programs rather than be doled out to individual unemployed and impoverished persons of both sexes. Simply giving people money would 'kill the initiative and enterprise of young Canadians,' discouraging them from seeking work and raising themselves up by their own bootstraps. Making men work for their relief, on the other hand, preserved male honour by preserving the ideal of the male breadwinner.

Despite its best wishes, however, the government could not completely eliminate the dole. But while direct relief was a necessary evil, its worst effects could be countered by making it as demeaning as possible – particularly to men. As James Struthers shows, people who applied for direct aid had to prove they were absolutely destitute and had exhausted every possible financial resource of their own and of close relatives. Having a car, radio, telephone, bank account, or insurance policy would disqualify one's application for direct relief: these were items that could be sold, and the income used to support oneself. Given the normative status of the patriarchal family, simply applying for the dole was emasculating. As one relief administrator recalled, teary-eyed men signed up 'as though they were signing away their manhood, the right to be a husband and sit at the head of the table.'

Receiving direct relief was also a humiliating and invasive process for everyone who applied. In Hamilton, for example, relief inspectors visited the homes of prospective recipients, taking a survey of the contents, and recording the number and ages of family members. Families on the dole received two weeks' worth of supplies, the contents of which were carefully recorded on ledger sheets, one kept by the family and another by the relief office. To get them, the unemployed lined up for hours at the relief office. Subsequent requests by the family for more supplies were assessed with reference to the ledger sheet. Here were surveillance tactics the Mounties would have been proud of.

Among the first people put out of work by the Great Depression were the thousands of transient, single young men. Many municipalities refused to grant them relief because they were not residents. In response, they rode the rods, searching for a town or city that would. The government viewed this floating population with alarm. Unconstrained by any responsibilities – to wives, families, or employers – they would gravitate towards the left, quickly becoming the dupes of 'Bolshevik' agitators. In the face of this 'menace to peace and safety,' in 1931 the federal government created relief camps for single men, administered, notably, by the Department of Defence, and located in the remotest parts of each province, as if they were modern-day penal colonies. There, out of harm's way, they were issued army-surplus uniforms, subjected to military discipline, and put to work building roads and airstrips or clearing brush, all for the princely sum of twenty cents a day. In forcing single unemployed men into these 'slave camps,' as the inmates called them, the government engaged in a kind of internal deportation, forcibly moving a part of the population it deemed dangerous, not because of their actions, but because of their status as poor single men who lived beyond the control of family and community.

Recognizing the emotive power of the family, those who criticized the relief camps publicized the plight of the inmates by recasting them as 'our boys': the men who were sent to the camps were not vagrants and bums, but sons and brothers who deserved to be treated as family members. More broadly, there was a sense that 'slave camps' were an affront to white-male dignity. Restriction to reserves might be appropriate for Indians, and internment at hard labour might be justified for 'dangerous foreigners' during a wartime crisis, but not for 'white men' during a different, though still severe, international economic crisis. In Vancouver, these racially loaded appeals worked. Citizens rallied around the relief camp workers and supported their 1935 strike and their bid to go 'on to Ottawa' to plead their case to R.B. Bennett. Though the government broke up their trek in Regina, the opposition to this coercive form of relief was so great that the camps were dismantled in 1936. While the successful protest against relief camps and the heroic On-to-Ottawa trek inspired widespread sympathy, the wartime and Depression-era internment of supposedly dangerous foreigners provoked no such response. Once again, it is clear that promoters of moral regulation were always at their most apologetic when the restrictions they imposed affected white men – people whose citizenship and rights were considered inviable.

Beyond enforcing gender norms, relief had a wider disciplinary function, exemplified by the principle that governed both the amount and the kind of aid individuals received: the principle of 'less eligibility.' Relief could not provide unemployed people with a better standard of living than that possible in the most menial of jobs. Otherwise, there would be little incentive for the unemployed to find work, and the government would be swamped with even more requests for funding. Thus, the ideal level of relief would give people a bare subsistence while still encouraging them to seek employment actively. In practice, less eligibility meant that families on relief could not expect the government to pay for medical care, clothing, soap, toiletries, or, in many cases, rent. Many municipalities expected reliefers to haggle with their landlords, somehow convincing them to forgo their rent, or at least delay it.

Moreover, some people were less eligible recipients than others. Married people were favoured over single ones, British subjects over others, and – in keeping with the old law of settlement – residents over transients. Those on the margin by virtue of their race or ethnicity suffered even more. Vancouver's relief administrator would not countenance the idea of giving the Chinese an equal amount of relief. Single Chinese men suffered a double liability and could expect help only from their own ethnic benevolent associations or the Anglican Church. It was not enough for 175 customers of one Pender Street soup kitchen, who starved to death between 1931 and 1935. For aboriginals, the privation of the Great Depression was nothing new. As one man recalled, 'We had our own little Depression around us like a chief's blanket all the time. If I'd have known then, I'd have had a few laughs knowing you people were getting it in the ass just like we had for fifty years. And more.'

In the end, the government failed to strike a balance between humanitarianism and discipline, and succeeded most in punishing the poor and unemployed. The federal government's insistence that relief was a provincial and municipal responsibility meant that it had no direct control over the distribution of its money. Federal money was distributed on the basis of a matching-grant formula rather than on the number of unemployed; thus, the most-well-off provinces and cities got the most money but had the fewest unemployed people to spend it on! This led to great disparities in relief payments: for instance, working-class Burnaby received $54,000, or $67.50 for each of its unemployed people, but in well-off West Vancouver, each of the thirty-five registered reliefers got $428.57. When it came to actually distributing relief to needy individuals, municipalities were further constrained by a shortage of trained staff and the absence of any overarching bureaucratic structure. As a result, each municipality ended up distributing relief through a loose collection of private charities, religious organizations, and newly formed relief committees. In Toronto, five private family charities worked with the city's Division of Social Welfare and the House of Industry to distribute relief. In Montreal things were worse: with no municipal social services, relief for the entire city was handled by four private religious charities. But the situation in Atlantic Canada was perhaps the most desperate, 'governed by Dickensian nineteenth-century principles.' Saint John residents who needed anything more than short-term relief were often placed in the city's Municipal Home, alongside the feeble-minded and infirm. Similarly in Nova Scotia, where it was illegal to give relief to the poor in their homes, the down and out were placed in the municipal poorhouses and their children 'placed elsewhere.'

Conclusion

The interwar period in Canada was characterized by a return to traditional political and ideological order. Dissent in the form of radical politics or simply being unemployed was labelled as immoral because it raised questions about justice of the capitalist order. The federal government took steps to stifle it by deporting the most visible advocates of dissent, members of the Communist Party of Canada, and then by dumping out the more numerous unemployed. In doing so, they were aided by the new and improved Mounties, an amended criminal code that made certain kinds of political dissent illegal, and an amended immigration act which legalized the deportation of dissenters. Since Confederation, the control of immigration had always been considered the key to making a moral dominion – whether that involved screening who came in or forcibly returning the 'unfit.' The unemployed who could not be deported were subjected to a system of relief shaped by prevailing assumptions about gender, marital status, residence, race, and ethnicity. The overriding concern was less to feed the hungry than to ensure that those who were fed were not corrupted in the bargain. At relief offices all over country, Canada's prisoners of starvation were guaranteed to get their fill of moralizing, if nothing else.

Conclusion

While we have not recounted every conceivable story of legal moral regulation, we have illustrated that the overarching aim of Canadian laws regarding morality was to forge a nation by making good its citizens. Officially successful in achieving this goal, but frequently futile in reality, it was a project rife with irony and contradiction.

Consolidating a group of colonies into a new dominion initiated a project of nation-building. The definition of moral standards for the nation was as important as building a transcontinental railway, if less celebrated. Young Canada was often portrayed as a virginal woman or as a sturdy young frontiersman: in both cases, the ideals of purity, industry, piety, and self-discipline were celebrated as essential features of Canadianness.

Following these ideals meant setting standards for citizenship as well as the nature of economic development. A range of departments and agencies, including the Department of Indian Affairs, the Ministry of Justice, and the North-West Mounted Police were established to frame the nation in an attempt to foster both economic and moral development. At local levels, police forces, schools, and correctional institutions developed in conjunction with factories as work discipline and moral discipline converged. By the 1890s, both federal and provincial legislation had moulded morality into the legal framework of the Dominion.

With Laurier's election in 1896, Canada looked optimistically towards the twentieth century as a period of unrivalled prosperity and national development. At the same time a spirit of religious reform and secular progressivism inspired campaigns to shape progress along moral lines. Several branches of the Protestant churches were particularly visible in this movement, and an alliance between Methodists and Presbyterians became the most influential lobbying bloc on matters as wide-ranging as marriage, alcohol, seduction, and gambling. Through organizations such as the Lord's Day Alliance, powerful Christians assumed a central role in the campaign to make good citizens.

At the same time, the state retained the coercive powers thought necessary to enforce religiously inspired visions of morality. And it invented new agencies – juvenile and family courts and morality squads – to absorb moral projects previously assumed by philanthropists. The administrative apparatus of legal moral regulation was enhanced as the First World War greatly widened the state's scope of surveillance and regulation over matters ranging from venereal disease to political dissent. However, laws introduced 'for the duration' tended to linger long after the crisis of war had passed, thereby entrenching themselves as permanent features of the regulatory landscape.

The Winnipeg General Strike sent shockwaves through the Canadian economic and political establishment because it signalled that the war's end had not spelled a return to normalcy. As fears of foreigners and radicalism escalated, the new Royal Canadian Mounted Police were granted greater powers in an attempt to reassert the foundational ideals of purity and industry. Political and moral non-conformity were conflated, and the heterosexual family norm took on greater significance. It was an era when inexpensive material pleasures, from comic books to motion pictures, were available, yet subjected to restrictive morals laws. At the same time, flagrant violations and lackadaisical enforcement, most notably of alcohol laws, made a mockery of legal regulatory might.

The onset of the Depression reinvigorated state control over morality, however. Like the war, this unprecedented national crisis provided the impetus to tighten the net of moral regulation around potentially troublesome citizens. While deportation remained a potent tool, so were labour camps, vagrancy statutes, and relief schemes. Prior to the expansion of the welfare state in the post–Second-World War era, legal morals regulation remained the key means of making good citizens – whether they liked it or not.

Throughout the book, several themes have appeared and reappeared in different guises. First, drives to control the character of Canadian life were not conducted with equal success across the country. Since responsibility for criminal law policy lay with the federal government and enforcement with the provinces, there was considerable variation in the stringency and nature of morals enforcement from province to province. As uneven as moral regulation was across the Dominion, one region stands out as being consistently different: Quebec. Whereas formal efforts to enforce goodness increasingly fell under the purview of the state in all other provinces, moral regulation in Quebec retained its largely clerical character throughout our period. Because of Quebec's unique church–state relations, the Roman Catholic Church continued to wield tremendous influence in defining and regulating morality.

Differences were apparent at the local level as well. Certain cities, such as Montreal, Winnipeg, and Calgary, gained a reputation for being 'wide open' (particularly when it came to their tolerance of prostitution), while others, most notably Toronto, gained a reputation for stolidly staying the course of morality. Still, when it came to specific forms of morals violations, such as breaking laws against the illicit liquor trade, big cities could fade in importance, while rural areas in provinces such as Saskatchewan and New Brunswick emerged as centres of immorality.

Second, an obvious, yet often-ignored feature of Canadian morals legislation in the late nineteenth and early twentieth centuries was the enduring presence of the

United States. Impossible to ignore, the allegedly immoral states of the union spurred Canadian legislators, lobbyists, and law enforcement officers in their quest to preserve Canada from the deleterious effects of proximity with the republic. Ironically, Canadians did their part to corrupt their southern neighbours by providing a pipeline for illegal liquor sales during the U.S. prohibition era. Nevertheless, defining immorality as coming from somewhere else, either the United States or Europe, became integral to Canadian identity-formation.

At the same time that powerful Canadians worried about outsiders, aboriginal peoples received special attention as an important *internal* threat to the foundation of a moral nation. Accordingly, their centrality to the project of moral regulation is our third theme. Painted both as childish innocents, easily led astray by unscrupulous whites, and as inveterate 'savages,' wilfully resistant to the best efforts of missionaries and Indian agents bent on civilizing them, aboriginals were singled out for racially encoded morals regulation. In particular, the Indian Act in its various guises tied rights of citizenship to behaviour never demanded of non-Native persons: legal prescriptions regarding schooling, drinking, as well as dress and song were defined and enforced by clerical and state authorities who called for the assimilation of aboriginals into 'Canadian' society. It would be no exaggeration to suggest that assaults on Native cultures were waged, not just on battlefields and in inequitable treaty negotiations, but also through the legal regulation of morality.

In many ways, Canada's First Nations served as guinea pigs for moral regulation. The tactics developed to make them good were subsequently applied to others – industrial schooling standing out as the most prominent example – and the same dynamic of protection and control which justified the treatment of aboriginals was apparent in the moral regulation of non-Native women and children. Just as aboriginals could find themselves at the mercy of unscrupulous liquor-sellers, and hence had to be isolated on reserves, girls and women could not be left unescorted on streets or train stations, lest they be duped by white slavers. Similarly, urban 'waifs and strays' had to be rescued from the streets and placed in care lest they fall into the clutches of hardened criminals. The broad similarities in both the tactics employed in making good and the attitudes animating them suggest that moral regulation should be seen as a way of managing the marginal, whether that marginality was conferred by race, class, or gender.

Our focus on Canada's First Nations also suggests a fourth broad characteristic of moral regulation – namely, that morals offences are often status offences: offences defined not so much by what the individual in question has done, but by who he or she is, and where and when the offence occurred. For instance, aboriginals were singled out for differential treatment by the state simply by virtue of their 'Indianness.' Similarly, unescorted women seen out at night or in certain places – taverns, ice cream parlours, or parks – were seen to be prostitutes; and single unemployed men who protested the government's lack of action during the Depression were branded subversives, and likely Communists.

Fifth, the association of immorality with particular people in particular places meant that moral regulation was often expressed through the control of space. As we have seen, the federal government moved to put aboriginals on reserves and to restrict the movement of the Plains peoples with a pass system; the Mounties and the municipal police attempted to regulate prostitution by confining it to certain 'red light' districts; and cities such as Vancouver tried to suppress radicalism by controlling the streets, preventing open-air speeches.

As oppressive and invasive as legal moral regulation could be, however, what stands out is how difficult it was to achieve. First, because legal moral regulation often began with high hopes and lofty goals – for example, eradicating vice completely – it failed by its own standards. Second, making a moral dominion was expensive. Confronted with the economic realities of staffing a morality squad, building prisons, and deporting the unemployed, the state's moral agents often preferred to *manage* vice through a system of revenue-generating regulations such as licences and taxation, rather than to eradicate immorality outright. Only when public pressure was too great to ignore, as during the white slavery panics and the Red Scare, would state agents be moved to launch an all-out war against morals offenders. State officials also found that criminalizing certain kinds of immoral behaviour could create as many problems as it solved. The law against the potlatch was a case in point. Responding to pressure from Christian missionaries, the federal government amended the Indian Act in 1884, making potlatching a criminal offence. However, difficulties in enforcing the law against the ceremony proved so great that many of the people who had supported criminalization in the first place began to wonder whether, in passing an unenforceable law, they had not undermined the legitimacy of the entire legal system. Similarly, while making drink and school attendance matters of law signalled the state's commitment to making a moral dominion, widespread evasion threatened to compromise the standing and reputation of those charged with enforcement. In the end, the law sometimes constrained as much as it enabled regulators to make good.

Legislation aimed at making good also did not always regulate what or whom it appeared to target. As we have seen, temperance and prohibition legislation, though meant to change the drinking habits of all Canadians, was in practice enforced against the working class, and working-class men in particular. Similarly, the strictures against opium were principally a means of regulating the Chinese, while laws attacking prostitution ended up casting doubt on the character and reputations of all women found out on the streets alone.

Perhaps the most significant obstacle to making good was the resistance that morals laws inspired. Not all Canadians shared the same vision of morality, and many took issue with attempts to make them citizens of the moral dominion. Whether it was attacking the police, as working-class Montrealers did in the anti-vaccination riots; stomping a Salvation Army officer's drum to bits in response to one-too-many lectures on temperance; continuing to speak in their own tongue, as many residential school students did; or simply lying to factory inspectors, truant officers, or judges, many people continued to assert their own sense of right and wrong, despite what they were told by the powerful and dominant. If resistance was assured, the success of moral regulation was not. Notions of goodness were contested, perpetually being made and unmade in the moral dominion.

References

Chapter 1 Building the Moral Dominion

Backhouse, Constance 'Nineteenth-Century Canadian Prostitution Law: Reflection of a Discriminatory Society.' *Histoire sociale/Social History* 18 (1985), 387–423
– 'Nineteenth-Century Canadian Rape Law, 1800–92.' In *Essays in the History of Canadian Law*, vol. 2, ed. D.H. Flaherty. Toronto, 1983
– '"Pure Patriarchy": Nineteenth-Century Canadian Marriage.' *McGill Law Journal* 31 (1986), 264–312
Baehre, Rainer. 'Prison as Factory, Convict as Worker: A Study of the Mid-Victorian St John Penitentiary, 1841–1880.' In *Essays in the History of Canadian Law*, vol. 5: *Crime and Criminal Justice*, ed. J. Phillips, T. Loo, and S. Lewthwaite. Toronto, 1994
Barman, Jean. 'Separate and Unequal: Indian and White Girls at All Hallows School, 1884–1920.' In *Indian Education in Canada*, Vol. 1: *The Legacy*. Vancouver, 1986
Barman, Jean, Yvonne Hébert, and Don McCaskill, eds. *Indian Education in Canada*. Vol. 1: *The Legacy*. Vancouver, 1986
Brown, Desmond. *The Genesis of the Canadian Criminal Code of 1892*. Toronto, 1989
Craven, Paul. 'Workers' Conspiracies in Toronto, 1854–72.' *Labour/Le Travail* 14 (1984), 49–70
Curtis, Bruce. *Building the Educational State: Canada West, 1836–1871*. London, Ont., 1988
Dubinsky, Karen, '"Maidenly Girls" or "Designing Women"? The

Crime of Seduction in Turn-of-the-Century Ontario.' In
Gender Conflicts: New Essays in Women's History, ed. F. Iacovetta
and M. Valverde. Toronto, 1992

Greer, Allan. 'From Folklore to Revolution: Charivaris and the
Lower Canadian Rebellion of 1837.' *Social History* 15 (1990),
25–43

Horrall, S.W. '"A policeman's lot is not a happy one": The
Mounted Police and Prohibition in the North West Territories, 1874–91.' *Transactions of the Historical and Scientific Society
of Manitoba* 30 (1974), 5–16

Macleod, R.C. 'Canadianizing the West: The North-West
Mounted Police as Agents of the National Policy, 1873–1905.'
In *The Prairie West: Historical Readings*, ed. R.D. Francis and
H. Palmer. Edmonton, 1985

– *The North-West Mounted Police and Law Enforcement, 1873–1905.*
Toronto, 1976

Marks, Lynne. 'Religion, Leisure, and Working-Class Identity.' In
Labouring Lives: Work and Workers in Nineteenth-Century Ontario,
ed. P. Craven. Toronto, 1995

Marquis, Greg. '"A Machine of Oppression under the Guise of
Law": The Saint John Police Establishment, 1860–1890.' In
Historical Perspectives on Law and Society in Canada, ed. T. Loo
and L. Maclean. Toronto, 1994

Miller, J.R. 'Owen Glendower, Hotspur, and Canadian Indian
Policy.' In *Sweet Promises: A Reader on Indian–White Relations in
Canada*, ed. J.R. Miller. Toronto, 1990

– *Shingwauk's Vision: A History of Native Residential Schools.*
Toronto, 1996

– *Skyscrapers Hide the Heavens: A History of Indian–White Relations
in Canada.* Rev. ed. Toronto, 1991

Morton, W.L. 'Manitoba Schools and Canadian Nationality,
1890–1923.' Canadian Historical Association *Report* 1951, 51–9

Noel, Jan. *Canada Dry: Temperance Crusades before Confederation.*
Toronto, 1995

Oliver, Peter. '"A Terror to Evil-Doers": The Central Prison and
the "Criminal Class" in Late-Nineteenth Century Ontario.' In
Patterns of the Past: Interpreting Ontario's History, ed. R. Hall, W.
Westfall, and L.S. MacDowell. Toronto, 1988

Palmer, Bryan D. 'Discordant Music: Charivaris and Whitecapping in Nineteenth-Century North America.' *Labour/Le Travailleur* 3 (1978), 5–62

Parker, Graham. 'The Legal Regulation of Sexual Activity and the Protection of Females.' *Osgoode Hall Law Journal* 21 (1983), 187–244

Prentice, Alison. *The School Promoters: Education and Social Class in Mid-Nineteenth Century Upper Canada.* Toronto, 1977

Stone, Thomas. 'The Mounties as Vigilantes: Perceptions of Community and the Transformation of Law in the Yukon, 1885–1897.' *Law and Society Review* 14 (1979), 83–114

Tobias, John L. 'Protection, Civilization, Assimilation: An Outline History of Canada's Indian Policy.' *The Western Journal of Anthropology* 6/2 (1976), 12–30

Tucker, Eric. '"That Indefinite Area of Toleration": Criminal Conspiracy and Trade Unions in Ontario, 1837–77.' *Labour/Le Travail* 27 (1991), 15–54

Walden, Keith. *Visions of Order.* Toronto, 1982

Chapter 2 Instituting Morality

Backhouse, Constance. 'Nineteenth-Century Canadian Prostitution Law: Reflection of a Discriminatory Society.' *Histoire sociale/Social History* 18 (1985), 387–423

– 'Nineteenth-Century Canadian Rape Law, 1800–92.' In *Essays in the History of Canadian Law*, vol. 2, ed. D.H. Flaherty. Toronto, 1983

– *Petticoats and Prejudice: Women and the Law in Nineteenth-Century Canada.* Toronto, 1991

Barman, Jean. 'Separate and Unequal: Indian and White Girls at All Hallows School, 1884–1920.' In *Indian Education in Canada*, vol. 1: *The Legacy*. Vancouver, 1986

Barron, F. Laurie. 'The Indian Pass System in the Canadian West, 1882–1935.' *Prairie Forum* 13 (Spring 1988), 25–42

Bennett, Paul W. 'Turning "Bad Boys" into "Good Citizens": The Reforming Impulse in Toronto's Industrial Schools Movement, 1883 to the 1920s.' *Ontario History* 78 (1986), 209–32

Betke, Carl. 'Pioneers and the Police on the Canadian Prairies,

1885–1914.' In *Lawful Authority: Readings on the History of Criminal Justice in Canada*, ed. R.C. Macleod. Toronto, 1988

Boritch, Helen, and John Hagan. 'Crime and the Changing Forms of Class Control: Policing Public Order in "Toronto the Good."' *Social Forces* 66 (1987), 307–35

Carter, Sarah. *Lost Harvests: Prairie Indian Reserve Farmers and Government Policy*. Kingston and Montreal, 1990

Cole, Douglas, and Ira Chaikin. *An Iron Hand upon the People: The Law against the Potlatch on the Northwest Coast*. Vancouver, 1990

Dubinsky, Karen. *Improper Advances: Rape and Heterosexual Conflict in Ontario, 1880–1929*. Chicago, 1993

Friesen, Gerald. *The Canadian Prairies: A History*. Toronto, 1987

Gaffield, Chad. 'Schooling, the Economy, and Rural Society in Nineteenth-Century Ontario.' In *Childhood and Family in Canadian History*, ed. J. Parr. Toronto, 1982

Heron, Craig. 'Factory Workers.' In *Labouring Lives: Work and Workers in Nineteenth-Century Ontario*, ed. P. Craven. Toronto, 1996

Horrall, S.W. '"A policeman's lot is not a happy one": The Mounted Police and Prohibition in the North West Territories, 1874–91.' *Transactions of the Historical and Scientific Society of Manitoba* 30 (1974), 5–16

– 'The (Royal) North-West Mounted Police and Prostitution on the Canadian Prairies.' *Prairie Forum* 10 (1985), 105–27

Hubner, Brian. 'Horse Stealing and the Borderline: The NWMP and the Control of Indian Movement, 1874–1900.' *Prairie Forum* 20/2 (Fall 1995), 281–300

Hurl, Lorna F. 'Restricting Child Factory Labour in Late-Nineteenth-Century Ontario.' *Labour/Le Travail* 21 (1988), 87–121

Jennings, John Nelson. 'The North West Mounted Police and Indian Policy, 1874–96.' Unpublished PhD diss., University of Toronto, 1979

Macleod, R.C. *The North West Mounted Police and Law Enforcement, 1873–1905*. Toronto, 1976

Marquis, Greg. '"A Machine of Oppression under the Guise of Law": The Saint John Police Establishment, 1860–1890.' In

Historical Perspectives on Law and Society in Canada, ed. T. Loo and L. Maclean. Toronto, 1994

Miller, J.R. 'Owen Glendower, Hotspur, and Canadian Indian Policy.' In *Sweet Promises: A Reader on Indian–White Relations in Canada,* ed. J.R. Miller. Toronto, 1990

– *Shingwauk's Vision: A History of Native Residential Schools.* Toronto, 1996

Splane, Richard B. *Social Welfare in Ontario, 1791–1893.* Toronto, 1965

Strange, Carolyn. 'The Velvet Glove: Maternalistic Reform at the Andrew Mercer Ontario Reformatory for Females, 1874–1927.' Unpublished MA thesis, University of Ottawa, 1983

Weaver, John C. *Crime, Constables, and Courts: Order and Transgression in a Canadian City, 1816–1970.* Montreal and Kingston, 1995

Chapter 3 Recruiting the State

Bennett, Paul W. 'Turning "Bad Boys" into "Good Citizens": The Reforming Impulse of Toronto's Industrial Schools Movement, 1883 to the 1920s.' *Ontario History* 78/3 (1986), 209–32

Brown, Robert Craig, and Ramsay Cook. *Canada 1896–1921: A Nation Transformed.* Toronto, 1974

Cook, Sharon Anne. *'Through Sunshine and Shadow': The Woman's Christian Temperance Union, Evangelism, and Reform in Ontario, 1874–1930.* Montreal, 1995

Gray, James H. *Booze: When Whisky Ruled the West.* Saskatoon, 1995 [1972]

– *Red Lights on the Prairies.* Saskatoon, 1971

Hallowell, Gerald A. *Prohibition in Ontario, 1919–1923.* Ottawa, 1972

McLaren, John. 'Chasing the Social Evil: Moral Fervour and the Evolution of Canada's Prostitution Laws, 1867–1917.' *Canadian Journal of Law and Society* 1 (1986), 125–65

Meen, Sharon Patricia, 'The Battle for the Sabbath: The Sabbatarian Lobby in Canada, 1890–1912.' Unpublished PhD diss., University of British Columbia, 1979

Smart, Reginald, and Alan C. Ogborne. *Northern Spirits: Drinking in Canada Then and Now.* Toronto, 1986

Snell, James G. 'The "White Life for Two": The Defence of Marriage and Sexual Morality in Canada, 1890–1914.' *Histoire sociale/Social History* 16 (May 1983), 111–28

Solomon, R., and M. Green. 'The First Century: The History of Nonmedical Opiate Use and Control Policies in Canada, 1870–1970.' *University of Western Ontario Law Review* 20/2 (1982), 307–36

Strange, Carolyn. 'From Modern Babylon to a City Upon a Hill: The Toronto Social Survey (1915) and the Search for Sexual Order in the City.' In *Patterns of the Past: Interpreting Ontario's History,* ed. Roger Hall, Laurel Sefton McDowell, and William Westfall. Toronto, 1988

Valverde, Mariana. *The Age of Light, Soap, and Water: Moral Reform in English Canada, 1885–1925.* Toronto, 1991

Chapter 4 Incorporating Moral Visions

Adams, Mary Louise, 'In Sickness and in Health: State Formation, Moral Regulation, and Early VD Initiatives in Ontario.' *Journal of Canadian Studies* 28 (Winter 1993/4), 117–30

Bedford, Judy. 'Prostitution in Calgary.' *Alberta History* 29/2 (1981), 1–11

Bennett, Paul W. 'Taming "Bad Boys" of the "Dangerous Class": Child Rescue and Restraint at the Victoria Industrial School 1887–1935.' *Social History/Histoire sociale* 21 (1986), 71–96

Bowker, Marjorie Montgomery 'Juvenile Court in Retrospect: Seven Decades of History in Alberta (1913–1984).' *Alberta Law Review* 24/2 (Winter 1986), 234–74

Buckley, Suzanne, and Janice Dickin McGinnis. 'Venereal Disease and Public Health Reform in Canada.' *Canadian Historical Review* 63/3 (1982), 110–28

Carrigan, D. Owen. *Crime and Punishment in Canada: A History.* Toronto, 1991

Cassel, Jay. *The Secret Plague: Venereal Disease in Canada, 1838–1939.* Toronto, 1987

Chapman, Terry L. 'An Oscar Wilde Type: "The Abominable Crime of Buggery" in Western Canada, 1890–1920.' *Criminal Justice History* 4 (1984), 97–118

– 'Sex Crimes in the West, 1890–1920.' *Alberta History* 35/4 (1987), 6–21

Chunn, Dorothy. *From Punishment to Doing Good: Family Courts and Socialized Justice in Ontario, 1880–1940.* Toronto, 1992

Gray, James H. *Booze: When Whisky Ruled the West.* Saskatoon, 1995 [1972]

Kinsman, Gary. *The Regulation of Desire: Homo and Hetero Sexualities,* 2d ed. Montreal, 1996

Marks, Lynne. 'Religion, Leisure, and Working-Class Identity.' In *Labouring Lives: Work and Workers in Nineteenth-Century Ontario,* ed. P. Craven. Toronto, 1995

Marquis, Greg. 'Vancouver Vice: The Police and the Negotiation of Morality, 1904–1935.' In *Essays in the History of Canadian Law: British Columbia and the Yukon,* ed. Hamar Foster and John McLaren. Toronto, 1995

Maynard, Steven. 'Through a Hole in the Lavatory Wall: Homosexual Subcultures, Police Surveillance, and the Dialectics of Discovery, Toronto, 1890–1930.' *Journal of the History of Sexuality* 5/2 (1994), 207–41

McLaren, John. 'White Slavers: The Reform of Canada's Prostitution Laws and Patterns of Enforcement, 1900–1920.' *Criminal Justice History* 8 (1987), 125–65

Myers, Tamara. 'Criminal Women and Bad Girls: Regulation and Punishment in Montreal, 1890–1930.' Unpublished PhD diss., McGill University, 1996

Jones, Andrew, and Leonard Rutman. *In the Children's Aid: J.J. Kelso and Child Welfare in Ontario.* Toronto, 1981

Stephen, Jennifer. 'The "Incorrigible," the "Bad," and the "Immoral": Toronto's Factory Girls and the Work of the Toronto Psychiatric Clinic.' In *Law, Society and the State: Essays in Modern Legal History,* ed. L.A. Knafla and S. Binnie. Toronto, 1995

Strange, Carolyn. *Toronto's Girl Problem: The Perils and Pleasures of the City, 1880–1930.* Toronto, 1995

Thorner, Thomas, and Neil B. Watson. 'Keeper of the King's
    Peace: Colonel G.E. Sanders and the Calgary Police Magis-
    trate's Court, 1911–1932.' *Urban History Review* 12/3 (1984),
    45–55
Weaver, John. *Crime, Constables, and Courts: Order and Transgres-
    sion in a Canadian City, 1816–1970.* Montreal and Kingston,
    1995

Chapter 5 Returning to Normalcy

Avery, Donald. *Reluctant Host: Canada's Response to Immigrant
    Workers, 1896–1994.* Toronto, 1995
Backhouse, Constance. 'White Female Help and Chinese-
    Canadian Employers: Race, Class, Gender and Law in the
    Case of Yee Clun, 1924.' *Canadian Ethnic Studies* 26–3 (1994),
    34–52
Chapman, Terry. 'The Anti-Drug Crusade in Western Canada,
    1885–1925.' In *Law and Society in Canada in Historical Perspec-
    tive*, ed. David Bercuson and Louis Knafla. Calgary, 1980
Chunn, Dorothy. *From Punishment to Doing Good: Family Courts
    and Socialized Justice in Ontario, 1880–1940.* Toronto, 1992
Dickinson, Harley D. 'Scientific Parenthood: The Mental
    Hygiene Movement and the Reform of Canadian Families,
    1925–1950.' *Journal of Comparative Family Studies* 24 (Autumn
    1993), 387–402
Dodd, Diane. 'The Birth Control Movement on Trial,
    1936–1937.' *Social History/Histoire sociale* 32 (November 1983),
    381–400
Dowbiggan, Ian. '"Keeping This Young Country Sane": C.K.
    Clarke, Immigration Restriction, and Canadian Psychiatry,
    1890–1925.' *Canadian Historical Review* 76/4 (December 1995),
    598–627
Dyck, Noel. *What Is the Indian 'Problem'? Tutelage and Resistance in
    Canadian Indian Administration.* St John's, 1991
Gray, James H. *Bacchanalia Revisited: Western Canada's Boozy Skid
    to Social Disaster.* Saskatoon, 1982
Guest, Dennis. *The Emergence of Social Security in Canada,* 2d ed.
    Vancouver, 1985

Heap, Ruby 'La Ligue de l'Enseignement (1902–1904): Héritage du Passé et Nouveaux Défis.' *Revue d'histoire de l'Amérique française* 36/3 (December 1982), 339–73

Lee, Victor. 'The Laws of Gold Mountain: A Sampling of Early Canadian Laws and Cases that Affected People of Chinese Ancestry.' *Manitoba Law Journal* 21 (1992), 301–24

Lévesque, Andrée. *Making and Breaking the Rules: Women in Québec, 1919–39.* Trans. Yvonne M. Klein. Toronto, 1994

Little, Margaret. 'Manhunts and Bingo Blabs: The Moral Regulation of Ontario Single Mothers.' In *Studies in Moral Regulation,* ed. Mariana Valverde. Toronto, 1994

Loo, Tina. 'Dan Cranmer's Potlatch: Law as Coercion, Symbol and Rhetoric.' *Canadian Historical Review* 73/2 (1992), 125–65

McCallum, Margaret. 'Keeping Women in Their Place: The Minimum Wage in Canada, (1910–25).' *Labour/Le Travail* 17 (Spring 1986), 29–58

McLaren, Angus, and Arlene Tigar McLaren. *Our Own Master Race: Eugenics in Canada, 1885–1945.* Toronto, 1990

– *The Bedroom and the State: The Changing Practices and Politics of Contraception and Abortion in Canada, 1880–1986.* Toronto, 1986

McLaren, John. 'Creating "Slaves of Satan" or "New Canadians"? The Law, Education, and the Socialization of Doukhobor Children, 1911–1935.' In *Essays in the History of Canadian Law: British Columbia and the Yukon,* ed. Hamar Foster and John McLaren. Toronto, 1995

Miller, J.R. *Shingwauk's Vision: A History of Native Residential Schools.* Toronto, 1996

Moscovitch, Allan, and Jim Albert, eds. *The Benevolent State: The Growth of Social Welfare in Canada.* Toronto, 1987

Owen, Wendy, and J.M. Bumsted. 'Divorce in a Small Province: A History of Divorce on Prince Edward Island from 1833.' *Acadiensis* 20/2 (1991), 86–104

Roberts, Barbara. *Whence They Came: Deportation from Canada, 1900–1935.* Ottawa, 1988

Rooke, Patricia T., and R.L. Schnell. *Discarding the Asylum: From Child Rescue to the Welfare State in English-Canada (1800–1950).* Lanham, Md., 1983

Snell, James G. 'Courts of Domestic Relations: A Study of Early-

Twentieth-Century Judicial Reform in Canada.' *Windsor Yearbook of Access to Justice* 6 (1986), 36–60

– *In the Shadow of the Law: Divorce in Canada, 1900–1939.* Toronto, 1991

– 'Regulating Nuptuality: Restricting Access to Marriage in Early Twentieth-Century English-Speaking Canada.' *Canadian Historical Review* 69 (December 1988), 466–89

Titley, E. Brian. *A Narrow Vision: Duncan Campbell Scott and the Administration of Indian Affairs in Canada.* Vancouver, 1986

Chapter 6 The Moral Crises of Capital

Avery, Donald H. *'Dangerous Foreigners': European Immigrant Workers and Labour Radicalism in Canada, 1896–1932.* Toronto, 1979

– *Reluctant Host: Canada's Response to Immigrant Workers, 1896–1994.* Toronto, 1995

Berton, Pierre. *The Great Depression, 1929–1939.* Toronto, 1990

Betcherman, Lita-Rose. *The Swastika and the Maple Leaf: Fascist Movements in Canada in the Thirties.* Toronto, 1975

Brown, Lorne. *When Freedom Was Lost: The Unemployed, the Agitator, and the State.* Montreal and Buffalo, 1987

Hannant, Larry. *The Infernal Machine: Investigating the Loyalty of Canada's Citizens.* Toronto, 1995

Imai, Shin. 'Deportation in the Depression.' *Queen's Law Journal* 7 (1981), 66–94

Mackenzie, J.B. 'Section 98, Criminal Code and Freedom of Expression in Canada.' *Queen's Law Journal* 4 (1972), 469–83

Roberts, Barbara. *Whence They Came: Deportation from Canada, 1900–1935.* Ottawa, 1988

Sangster, Joan. *Dreams of Equality: Women on the Canadian Left, 1920–1950.* Toronto, 1983

Struthers, James. *No Fault of Their Own: Unemployment and the Canadian Welfare State, 1914–1941.* Toronto, 1983

Sweatman, Margaret. *Fox.* Winnipeg, 1991

Thompson, John Herd, with Allen Seager. *Canada, 1922–1939: Decades of Discord.* Toronto, 1985

Index

aboriginals: alcohol regulation and, 75, 90; capitalism, imposition on, 10; citizenship and, 114; civilizing of, 25, 43–4; farming and, 43–6; federal authority for, 25; gender roles of, 45; horse-stealing, 41; industrial schools and *(see* industrial schools); languages of, 48; missionaries and, 45, 75; moral regulation of, 46, 148; mother's allowance exclusion, 111; Mounties and, 22, 40–2; pass system and, 41, 44, 47; Plains Nations, treaty negotiations with, 41; potlatching, 45–7, 117–18; private property and, 44; reserve system and, 25, 41; resistance by, 47; schooling of *(see* industrial schools; residential schools); threat to Euro-Canadians, 46–7; tribal system of, 44; West Coast, common-property notions of, 44; —, potlatch, 45, 47; *see also* Department of Indian Affairs; Indian Act

abortion, 112–13

alcohol: aboriginals and, 75, 90; consumption of, 5–6, 32, 70–1; ethnicity and arrest, 88–9; licensing of, 91; national plebiscite on prohibition, 72; prohibition, 88–9; prostitution, relation to, 69–70; restrictions of, 74; Royal Commission on the Liquor Traffic, 70–1, 72; taverns, 33, 74–5; trade *(see* Royal Northwest Mounted Police); Woman's Christian Temperance Union campaign, 71–3; *see also* temperance

Andrew Mercer Ontario